D0323571

The Easy Way to WILD FLOWER Recognition

John Kilbracken

Kingfisher Books

The author wishes to thank Dr Bob Press of
the Natural History Museum and Dr Tom Cope
of the Royal Botanic Gardens for their help
in the preparation of this book.

First published in 1984 by Kingfisher Books Limited
Elsley Court, 20-22 Great Titchfield Street
London W1P 7AD

Text Copyright © John Kilbracken 1984
Illustrations Copyright © Kingfisher Books 1984

All Rights Reserved

BRITISH LIBRARY CATALOGUING IN PUBLICATION DATA
Kilbracken, John Godley, *Baron*
The easy way to wild flower recognition.
1. Wild flowers–Great Britain
I. Title
582.13'0941 QK306
ISBN 0 86272 088 5

Illustrations by Wendy Bramall and Shirley Willis
Phototypeset by Southern Positives and Negatives (SPAN)
Lingfield, Surrey
Colour separations by Newsele Litho Ltd, Milan, London
Printed in Italy by Vallardi Industrie Grafiche, Milan

How to Use this Book

This book has been written with only one end in view – to help the beginner to identify, more easily than ever before, the wild flowers most likely to be seen in Britain and Ireland. It does this in a way that is quite different from all the other flower identification books available. With the other books, unless you know the family to which the flower you have seen belongs, you must go through the whole volume looking at the illustrations and reading often complex descriptions until you decide which is the right one.

In *The Easy Way to Wild Flower Recognition*, you are led through the book by a number of simple questions about the flower you are identifying, till you quickly arrive at the answer. It is a companion volume to my two earlier books, *The Easy Way to Bird Recognition* and *The Easy Way to Tree Recognition*, which used precisely the same technique for identifying birds and trees.

If you glance at the text, you will see that it consists of a series of Questions and Answers, numbered consecutively from 1 to 373. The Questions are numbered in blue, the Answers in yellow. When you wish to identify a flower, always start at Question 1. Have a look at it now: it asks you what colour the flower is. You should have little trouble in deciding on the correct reply, which directs you to the next Question. So you are led on, rather as though you were following the clues in a treasure hunt, towards identification. The Questions are extremely simply worded, and there is nearly always a passage of text and illustrations to help you choose your answer. All technical terms you might not know or understand have been avoided; or, if this sometimes proved impossible, they are carefully explained.

After perhaps as few as three Questions, and never more than a dozen, you'll find that you arrive at an Answer. Here the flower is illustrated in colour, with a passage of descriptive text giving details that will help in identification. The months when the flower is most likely to be in bloom are also given. In almost every case, each species has an Answer to itself, and your trail is at an end. Occasionally, where two species are very similar, they are taken together in the same Answer. Both species are illustrated, so you should have no trouble deciding between them.

Now let's see how the book works in practice, taking the daisy – a flower almost everyone knows already – as an example. Turn to Question 1: 'What colour are its flowers?' The daisy's petals are tipped with red and it has a yellow centre, but the text tells you clearly: 'If two or more colours are present, choose the one that is most noticeable.' There is no doubt, in the case of the daisy, that this is WHITE, and you are therefore directed at once to Question 87. This asks whether or not the plant grows in water. Since it does not, go on to 93. This asks you about the leaves – whether they are alternate, opposite, whorled or basal. If you don't know precisely what these words mean when applied to leaves, they are carefully explained in simple language, and illustrated, so you should see at once that the daisy's leaves are BASAL (meaning that they all grow at the base of the plant). You are then directed to 171.

The flowers grow SINGLY, which leads you to 172; they are REGULAR, which takes you to 173; and each flower has MORE THAN SIX PETALS, which brings you on to 182. This, after a 'treasure-trail' of only six Questions, is your Answer. A read of the text and a look at the illustration should leave you in no doubt that you have identified the flower correctly.

If you happen to arrive at an Answer that is clearly incorrect, there are only two possible explanations. Either you have made a mistake somewhere along the line, and should go back to the beginning and try again, or you have come across a flower not common enough to be included in the book. It would have been impossible to include all those you might come across, so I decided to limit the number to the 200 commonest species. This was not an easy task. It may sometimes happen that a flower found quite often in your particular neighbourhood, or in a stretch of the country you visit, is not among them. In such cases you should consult a more comprehensive guide. But the chosen species should cover all those beginners are most likely to see in their first year or two, unless they are specially lucky.

In some ways, this book should be far easier to use than its predecessors on trees and birds. Flowers are much more distinctive than leaves – on which I mainly relied in the tree book – and they vary very little in colour, size and shape. Exceptions to this rule, like the flowers of the comfrey, which may be white, bluish-purple or pink, have been taken into account, and you will arrive at comfrey whether you choose white, red or blue as your answer to Question 1, though by completely different routes. Unlike a bird, a plant stays put and you have all the time in the world to examine it closely, to take measurements if necessary, and to check all minor details.

I should like to recommend that you slip this book in your pocket and take it with you when you are out looking for flowers, rather than picking the flowers and bringing them back to identify at home. In the case of certain rare species, it is against the law to do so. It is always against the law to *dig up* wild flowers, roots and all, without the permission of the landowner. But as a general rule, you should not pick wild flowers unless they are of a species seen plentifully in the neighbourhood. Also, by taking the book to the flower, you ensure that the flower is fresh and therefore easier to identify, and that you have the whole plant available for inspection.

I have not included a glossary in the book because the few difficult words that are used (e.g. involucre, bract) are always explained when they occur. But one important point should be made in this connection. Some flowers – almost all daisy-like or dandelion-like – appear to have one or more rings of radiating petals. In fact these are *not* petals. Each of them is technically an individual flower known as a *ray floret*. However, in this book I treat them as petals, which they appear to be to a beginner. Any reference to petals should therefore be taken as including ray florets.

JK
Killegar
1984

1 What colour are its flowers?

In most cases the answer will be self-evident. If two or more colours are present, choose the one that is most noticeable.

It is only with purplish flowers that you may feel any doubt. Make it the rule to choose 'Red or reddish' if they are pink, purple-red, or any other colour that seems on balance closer to red than blue. Choose 'Blue or bluish' if they are violet, lilac, purple-blue, or any other colour that seems closer to blue than red.

Yellow [2]
White or greenish-white [87]
Red or reddish [192]
Blue or bluish [292]
Green or brown [342]

2 Is the plant growing in water?

(from 1)
Answer 'Yes' if the lower part of the stem, or all the stem, is submerged in water. Answer 'No' if the plant is growing on dry land, or if only the roots are submerged.

Yes [3] No [6]

3 Are the flowers regular?

(from 2)
Answer 'Yes' if all the petals of each flower are equal in size and the same shape. Otherwise answer 'No'.

Yes [4] No [5]

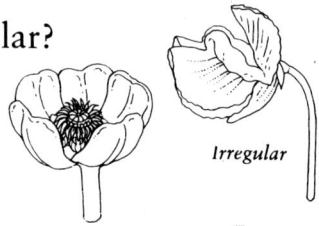

Irregular

Regular

4 YELLOW WATER-LILY *(Nuphar lutea)*

(from 3)

This water-lily always grows in still or slow-moving water. Its solitary flowers (4–6cm) have 5 petals and grow from stalks that usually rise a few inches above the water; but the large, glossy, heart-shaped leaves float flatly on the surface. Flowers June–August.

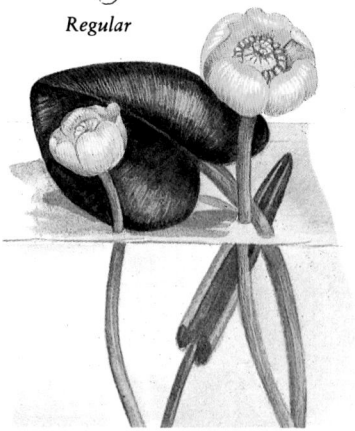

5 GREATER BLADDERWORT
(Utricularia vulgaris)

(from 3)

This rootless plant grows only in still water. Its flowers (12–15mm) grow alternately along the upper part of its erect stem, which also bears a few very small leaves, stalkless and alternate. Flowers July–September.

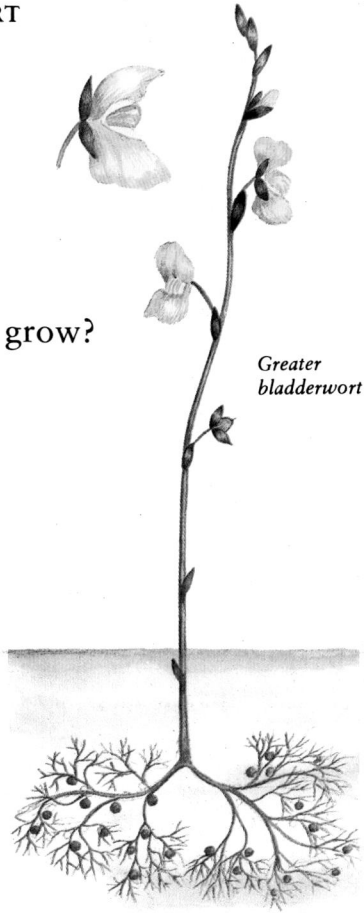

Greater bladderwort

6 How do the leaves grow?

(from 2)

Leaves are described as being alternate, opposite, whorled or basal, depending on how they grow along their stem or stalk.

Alternate leaves grow singly, on alternating sides of it. Opposite leaves are in pairs, and whorled leaves in groups of 3 or more around it. Choose 'Basal only' if all the leaves grow at the very base of the plant. Choose 'None visible' if no leaves are present when the flower is in bloom.

The drawings should make your choice quite easy.

Alternate [7]
Opposite or whorled [59]
Basal only [73]
None visible [86]

Alternate *Opposite* *Whorled* *Basal only*

7 Do the flowers lack petals?

(from 6)
This question needs no elaboration. Yes 8 No 15

8 Are the flowers very small?

(from 7)
Answer 'Yes' if the flowers are no more than 4mm in diameter. Otherwise answer 'No'.
Yes 9 No 12

9 Is the plant aromatic?

(from 8)
Answer 'Yes' if the leaves give off a pleasant aroma when crushed. Otherwise answer 'No'.

Yes 10 No 11

10 MUGWORT *(Artemisia vulgaris)*

(from 9)

The flowers are brownish yellow, bell-shaped and very small (3–4mm), growing in loose clusters at the end of the branching stems. The plant grows erect and may exceed 100cm in height. The stalkless leaves are deeply divided and clasp the stem. Mugwort is often found on dry wasteland and by roadsides. It flowers July–September.

11 **COMMON GROUNDSEL**
(Senecio vulgaris)
(from 9)

The undistinguished groundsel is a weed of wasteland and arable ground. Its very small flowers grow in loose clusters. The leaves are deeply lobed and are stalkless, grasping the stem, except at the base of the plant. Seldom exceeds 25cm in height. Flowers almost all year.

12 Are the flowers flat-topped?

(from 8)

Answer 'Yes' if the flowers (7–12mm) are flat-topped. Answer 'No' if they are rather smaller, and domed or rounded in shape.

Yes 13 No 14

Flat-topped flowers

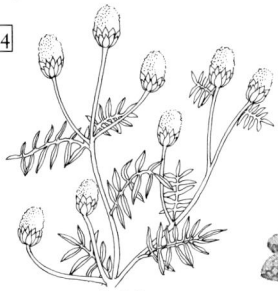

Rounded flowers

13 **TANSY**
(Tanacetum vulgare)
(from 12)

Tansy is distinguished by its button-like flowers, which have no radiating petals or florets. They grow in quite dense, flat-topped clusters, 7–15cm in diameter. The leaves are so deeply divided that they are almost fern-like; they are hairless and stalkless. Tansy grows on wasteland, by hedgerows or at roadsides. Flowers July–September.

14 **PINEAPPLEWEED**
(Matricaria matricarioides)
(from 12)

The flowers of pineappleweed (6–10mm) grow in small clusters on quite long individual stalks. The compound leaves are extremely deeply divided, so that they are almost fern-like. The plant grows erect and has a vague smell of pineapple if crushed. Usually found on pathways, tracks, or other trampled ground. Flowers June–July.

15 Are the flowers very large and showy?
(from 7)

Answer 'Yes' if the flowers are iris-like and very large (8–10cm), with 1–3 blooms on each flattened, erect stem. Otherwise answer 'No'.

Yes 16

No 17

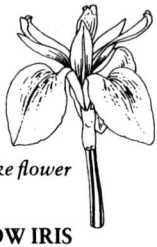

Iris-like flower

16 **YELLOW IRIS**
(Iris pseudacorus)
(from 15)

This tall, handsome plant is quite unmistakable. It reaches a height of 150cm and has large flowers up to 10cm in diameter. Their three larger petals alternate with three smaller ones. The very long, narrow leaves have conspicuous parallel veins. Yellow iris grows in moist or wet ground, often beside a river, and likes land that is flooded in winter. Flowers May–July.

17 Are the flowers regular?

(from 15)

Answer 'Yes' if all the petals of each flower are equal in size and the same shape; or, if there are two or more rings of petals in each flower, the petals in each ring are equal and the same shape. Otherwise answer 'No'.

Yes 18 No 51

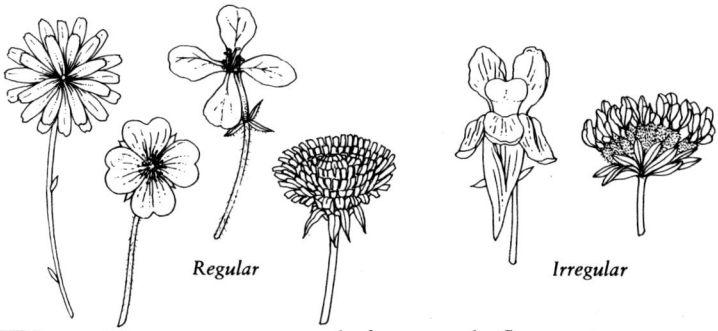

18 How many petals has each flower?

(from 17)

Count the number of petals in each flower and choose your answer accordingly.

4 19
5 27
6–12 42
Over 12 43

19 Are the leaves composite?

(from 18)

Answer 'Yes' if each leaf is composed of several separate leaflets. Answer 'No' if the leaves, though they may be deeply divided, are each single and independent.

Yes 20 No 23

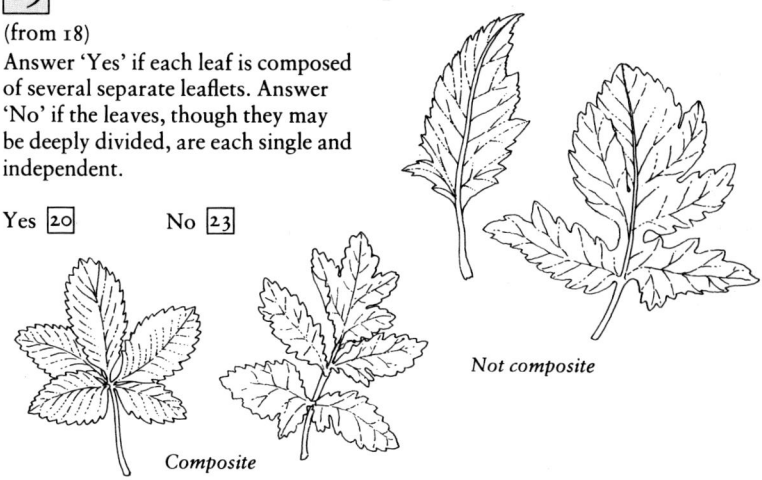

20 What size are the flowers?

(from 19)
Measure the diameter of an average-sized flower to decide which is the right answer.

2–2½cm [21]
Up to 1½cm [22]
Over 2½cm [117]

21 GREATER CELANDINE
(Chelidonium majus)

(from 20)

This is a member of the poppy family and is no relation to the well-known lesser celandine (see 74). It is a leafy plant with roughly toothed, almost hairless foliage. Its quite large flowers (about 2cm) are in clusters of 4–6. Often grows on walls, or on the banks of hedgerows. Flowers May–August.

22 TORMENTIL
(Potentilla erecta)

(from 20)

Tormentil usually grows more or less erect. It prefers acid soils and is found on fens and bogland as well as in fields. Its petals are roughly heart-shaped and only slightly longer than the narrow sepals between them. The leaves at the base of the plant have three leaflets and are stalked, whilst the upper leaves are stalkless and have 3–5 leaflets. Flowers June–September.

Greater celandine

Tormentil

23 What size are the flowers?

(from 19)

Measure the diameter of an average-sized flower to decide which is the right answer.

Over 5cm 24
About 2cm 25
Under 1cm 26

24 YELLOW HORNED POPPY
(Glaucium flavum)

(from 23)

Usually grows on or near the sea-shore. The conspicuous flowers (7–8cm) each have 4 delicate petals. The lower leaves are deeply lobed and have quite long, hairy stalks; the upper leaves are stalkless and their lobes are not so deep. Flowers June–October.

25 CHARLOCK
(Sinapis arvensis)

(from 23)

Charlock is a common weed on arable ground. Its bright yellow flowers grow in loose clusters at the tops of their stalks. The foliage is covered with rough hairs. The lower leaves have stalks and are deeply divided, whilst the upper ones are toothed and stalkless. Flowers May–July.

26 HEDGE MUSTARD
(Sisymbrium officinale)

(from 23)

This is a common plant on wasteland and is also found by roadsides or hedgerows or on arable land. Its very small flowers grow in quite long clusters. The lower leaves are deeply lobed with the largest lobe at the end; the upper leaves are more variable. The erect stem may reach a height of almost 100cm and has branching flower-stalks. Flowers May–September.

27 Are the leaves composite?

(from 18)

Answer 'Yes' if each leaf is composed of several separate leaflets. Answer 'No' if the leaves, though they may be deeply divided, are each single and independent.

Yes 28 No 31

Composite

Not composite

28 Do the flowers grow singly?

(from 27)

Answer 'Yes' if each flower is solitary, with its own stalk to itself. Answer 'No' if many flowers grow close together in a spike at the end of the stem.

Yes 29 No 30

Flowers single

Flowers in spike

29

SILVERWEED
(Potentilla anserina)

(from 28)

The leaves of silverweed are covered with silky hairs, especially the undersides, making them silver-white. Each leaf has many toothed leaflets, alternately quite large and very small. The plant grows in damp fields and on roadsides. Its flowers (10–18mm) have rounded petals. Never reaches a great height but sends out rooting runners up to almost 100cm in length. Flowers June–August.

30

COMMON AGRIMONY
(Agrimonia eupatoria)

(from 28)

This plant is to be found on roadsides, at the edge of meadows and in hedgerows. Its small flowers (5–8mm) form a regular spike several centimetres long. The undersides of the leaves are hairy and greyish. Each is composed of several quite large, toothed leaflets, alternating with smaller ones. Flowers June–August.

31

Is the plant growing in wet ground?

(from 27)

This question needs no elaboration.

Yes 32 No 35

32

Are the leaves heart-shaped?

(from 31)

Answer 'Yes' if the large, glossy leaves are noticeably heart-shaped. Otherwise answer 'No'.

Yes 33 No 34

33 MARSH-MARIGOLD
(Caltha palustris)
(from 32)

The conspicuous, glossy flowers of marsh-marigold or kingcup are large (3–5cm) and golden yellow. The toothed leaves are completely hairless, as is the hollow stem. This plant almost always grows in or near water or on very damp ground, often by a river. Flowers March–July.

Marsh-marigold

Lesser spearwort

34 LESSER SPEARWORT
(Ranunculus flammula)
(from 32)

Lesser spearwort is a member of the buttercup family, but differs from the others in having sharply pointed leaves that are not lobed or divided. Its flowers, which are 8–20mm in size, tend to be smaller than those of other buttercups and are less glossy. They grow in loose clusters, each with its own independent stalk. Found in damp places, often in ditches or beside water. Flowers May–September.

35 Does each flower have a noticeable stalk?

(from 31)

Answer 'Yes' if the flowers grow singly, or in loose clusters of 2–5 independent flowers, each with a definite stalk. Answer 'No' if they are arranged in clusters with many flowers that are stalkless or nearly so.

Yes 36 No 41

Flowers with stalks *Unstalked flowers*

36 Are the flowers a bright, glossy yellow?

(from 35)

Answer 'Yes' if it is a buttercup, with the well-known glossy yellow flowers. Otherwise answer 'No'.

Yes 37 No 38

37

(from 36)

MEADOW BUTTERCUP
(Ranunculus acris)
CREEPING BUTTERCUP
(Ranunculus repens)

These are the two commonest buttercups and they are so similar that it is best to consider them together. The main difference is that the flower-stalks of the meadow buttercup are smooth, whilst the creeping buttercup's are noticeably furrowed. The former is usually seen in open fields, whilst the latter is also found in damp ditches or by roadsides.

Creeping buttercup

Both species have conspicuous yellow flowers ($1\frac{1}{2}$–$2\frac{1}{2}$cm), deeply divided leaves and erect stems. (The creeping buttercup gets its name because it puts out many runners, which root at intervals.) Both flower April–September.

38 Is the plant fleshy?

(from 36)
Answer 'Yes' if the stems and leaves are hairless and noticeably fleshy, and the leaves have an unusual swollen shape. Otherwise answer 'No'.

Yes 39 No 40

Meadow buttercup

39 BITING STONECROP *(Sedum acre)*

(from 38)

The leaves of biting stonecrop, like those of other plants in the same family, are unusual in being plump and fleshy, without veins or stalks. The flowers grow in small clusters of 2–5. The plant is typically found growing on walls, or on dry, stony ground. Flowers June–July.

Biting stonecrop

40 HERB BENNET *(Geum urbanum)*

(from 38)

Herb bennet, as indicated by its other name,wood avens, is usually found in woods or shady hedgerows. Its flowers (10–18mm) grow in small, loose clusters, each with its own flower stalk. They have 5 prominent sepals, almost as long as the petals and at first visible between them, alternating with 5 shorter ones. Flowers June–August.

Herb bennet

Aaron's rod

41 **AARON'S ROD**
(Verbascum thapsus)
(from 35)

This plant, also known as great mullein, is distinguished by its soft, downy leaves. They are grey-white and mostly stalkless. It grows erect and may exceed 100cm in height, with a long regular spike of tightly-packed flowers. Often found on waste ground or dry roadsides, it flowers from June to August.

42 **GOLDENROD**
(Solidago virgaurea)
(from 18)

The flowers of goldenrod may have 6–12 petals, and are arranged in loose clusters around their stalks. The oval leaves are slightly toothed and almost stalkless. This plant has two quite different habitats: on high ground, where it may grow among mountain rocks to a maximum height of 20cm, and in lowland country, where it is found in hedgerows or woodland and may exceed 100cm. Flowers July–September.

Goldenrod

43 Do the flowers grow singly?

(from 18)

Answer 'Yes' if each flower is solitary, with its own stem to itself. Answer 'No' if many flowers grow close together in a spike or cluster at the end of the stem.

Yes 44 No 45

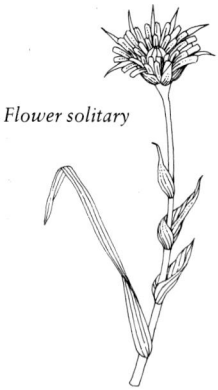

Flower solitary

Flowers in cluster

44 JACK-GO-TO-BED-AT-NOON

(Tragopogon pratensis)

(from 43)

The flower (4–5cm) is something like a dandelion's, but has long, narrow, sepal-like bracts, which spread out round it like the rays of the sun. The leaves are hairless and grass-like, grasping the stem. The plant gets its name from its flowers, which open in early morning and close around midday. It is also known as goat's-beard. Grows in wasteland or grassland; flowers June–July.

45 Is the stem hollow?

(from 43)

Cut the stem, or break it, to find out and choose your answer accordingly.

Yes 46 No 47

46 SMOOTH SOW-THISTLE
(Sonchus oleraceus)

(from 45)

The flowers (2–2½cm) are pale yellow and grow in loose clusters at the end of branching stems. The plant is erect and may exceed 100cm in height. All its leaves have rather spiny teeth; they are stalkless and grasp the stem at their bases. The lower leaves are deeply divided. This is a weed of wasteland, arable ground and roadsides, often growing near walls. Flowers June–August.

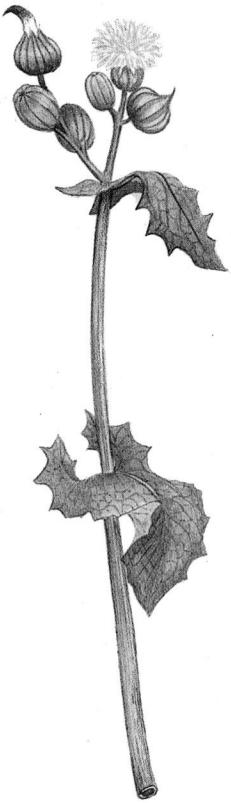

47 What shape are the leaves?

(from 45)

A lobe is a deep indentation in the margin of a leaf. You have to decide if the leaves are all without lobes, if those at the base of the plant are quite noticeably lobed, or if all the leaves are so deeply divided that each division almost forms a separate leaflet. The drawings should make it quite easy to decide.

All leaves unlobed 48
Basal leaves lobed 49
All deeply divided 50

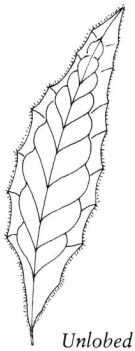

Unlobed

Lobed basal leaves

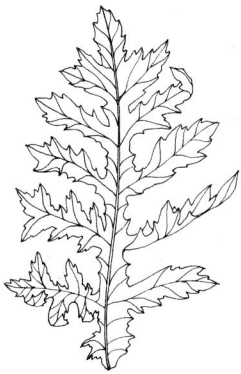

Deeply divided

48 HAWKWEED
(Hieracium)

(from 47)

The hawkweeds form a specially difficult group because up to 300 different species have been identified in the British Isles, some of them so similar that it takes an expert to distinguish them. They form a study in themselves and it is not intended to differentiate between them here.

All hawkweeds have flowers like small dandelions, arranged in loose clusters at the ends of usually unbranched stems. They normally have narrow, toothed leaves, which are hairy underneath and may or may not be stalked. The stems, too, are hairy, and give out a bitter, white liquid if cut or broken. Hawkweeds prefer some shade and are often found in open woodland, by roadsides or in hedgerows, but also in grassland. Flowers June–September.

49 NIPPLEWORT
(Lapsana communis)
SMOOTH HAWK'S-BEARD
(Crepis capillaris)

(from 47)

These two plants are quite similar and it is best to take them together. In both cases the flowers (1–2cm) are like small dandelions in loose clusters; and in both the upper leaves are very variable in shape. The most noticeable difference is the shape of the leaves at the base of the plant: those of nipplewort are roughly toothed, with one large lobe and two or more smaller ones, whilst hawk's-beard's are lobed more regularly along most of all of their length. Both grow on wasteland – nipplewort (flowers July–September) prefers shady ground, whilst hawk's-beard (flowers June–September) may grow in open fields.

Common ragwort

50 **COMMON RAGWORT**
(Senecio jacobaea)

(from 47)

Ragwort is a common weed of neglected grassland, which spreads rapidly and can take over large areas. Its bright yellow flowers ($1\frac{1}{2}$–$2\frac{1}{2}$cm) have up to a dozen radiating florets (which look like petals) and are arranged in quite close clusters at the ends of branching stems. The leaves are deeply divided, mostly stalkless, and hairless or nearly so. Flowers June–October.

51 Are the leaves composite?

(from 17)

Answer 'Yes' if each leaf is composed of several separate leaflets. Answer 'No' if the leaves, though they may be deeply divided, are each single and independent.

Yes 52 No 57

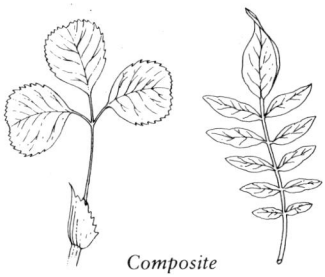

Composite

Not composite

52 Are the flowers woolly?

(from 51)

Answer 'Yes' if the green sepals at the base of each flower in the cluster are clothed with woolly white hair. Otherwise answer 'No'.

Yes 53 No 54

53 KIDNEY VETCH
(Anthyllis vulneraria)

(from 52)

This plant grows almost erect, with many closely-packed clusters of irregular flowers, shaped like those of a pea. Each flowerhead has its own stalk, and there is a ring of leaf-like bracts where it joins the flowerhead. The leaflets are arranged in pairs, with the largest one at the end, then becoming progressively smaller. Grows in dry grassland, often by the sea. Flowers June–August.

54 What size are the flowers?

(from 52)

Measure the diameter of an average-sized flower and decide on your answer accordingly.

10–15mm 55
2–3mm 56

55 BIRD'S-FOOT TREFOIL
(Lotus corniculatus)

(from 54)

Bird's-foot trefoil belongs to the pea family, and its flowers (1–1½cm long) have the unusual, irregular shape of those of other members of the family. Most of the stem lies prostrate, but the ends turn upward, bearing loose clusters of 2–7 bright yellow flowers. Normally grows in meadows and pasture. Flowers June–September.

56 BLACK MEDICK
(Medicago lupulina)

(from 54)

Each little flowerhead of black medick appears spherical in shape, but on examination is seen to consist of 10–50 tiny individual flowers (2–3mm). Each leaf is divided into three rounded, toothed leaflets, forming a classic trefoil, and there are two more leaflets at the base of each leaf-stalk. Black medick is a sprawling plant, but may sometimes approach 50mm in height. It is generally downy and produces black fruit. Usually found in grassy, open places. Flowers April–August.

57 Does each flower grow singly?

(from 51)

Answer 'Yes' if each flower grows independently on its own quite long stalk. Choose 'No' if the flowers are almost stalkless, in a tightly-grouped cluster.

Yes 327 No 58

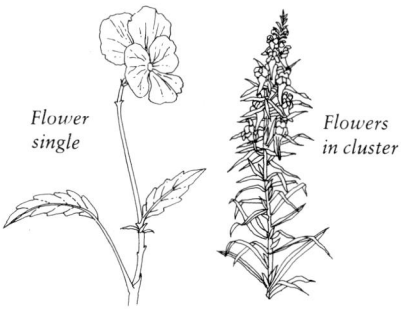

58 COMMON TOADFLAX
(Linaria vulgaris)

(from 57 and 71)

The leaves of common toadflax, which are long and narrow, may be alternate, opposite or whorled. The unusual irregular flowers ($1\frac{1}{2}$–$2\frac{1}{2}$cm long) are arranged in a long spike at the end of each flowering stem. The plant grows in grassland or by roadsides. Flowers June–December.

59 Are the flowers regular?

(from 6)

Answer 'Yes' if all the petals of each flower are equal in size and the same shape. Otherwise answer 'No'.

Yes 60 No 67

Regular

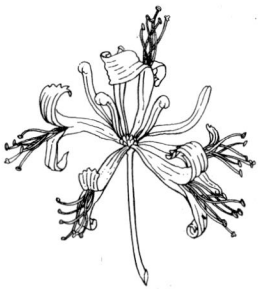

Irregular

60 How many petals has each flower?

(from 59)

Count the number of petals in each flower and choose your answer accordingly.

4 61
5 62

61 LADY'S BEDSTRAW *(Galium verum)*

(from 60)

This distinctive plant has perfectly regular, small flowers (2–4mm), growing in quite loose clusters at the ends of branching stems, which are square and rather hairy. The narrow leaves grow in whorls of 8–12. It thrives in dry, grassy land and in hedgerows or wasteland. Flowers July–August.

62 Is the plant prostrate?

(from 60)

Answer 'Yes' if, for most of its length, the stem is lying prostrate along the ground. Answer 'No' if it is erect.

Yes 63 No 64

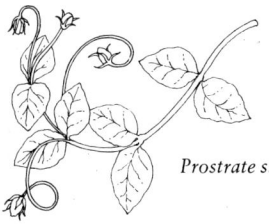

Prostrate stem

Erect stem

63 YELLOW PIMPERNEL *(Lysimachia nemorum)*

(from 62)

The little yellow flowers rise at intervals from the prostrate stem, each on its own stalk. There are noticeable green sepals alternating between the petals. The hairless, toothless leaves are shiny and oval with very short stalks. This plant prefers shade and grows in woodland or hedgerows. Flowers May–July.

64 Are the stems square?

(from 62)

Answer 'Yes' if the stem has four flanges or wings, so that it appears square in cross-section. Answer 'No' if it has only two flanges and they are less conspicuous.

Yes 65 No 66

Square stem

Rounded stem

65 SQUARE-STEMMED ST JOHN'S-WORT
(Hypericum tetrapterum)

(from 64)

Square-stemmed St John's-wort differs from its near relative perforate St John's-wort (see 66) mainly because of its square stem and smaller flowers (1cm). These grow in a loose cluster at the end of their stem. The plant rises erect and is hairless; it prefers damp ground and often grows near water. Flowers June–September.

Square-stemmed St John's-wort

Perforate St John's-wort

66 PERFORATE ST JOHN'S-WORT
(Hypericum perforatum)

(from 64)

In every way similar to square-stemmed St John's-wort (see 65), except for its larger flowers (2cm) and more rounded stalk.

67 Is the stem square?

(from 59)

You will have no difficulty deciding whether the stem is square, with four straight sides, instead of being rounded as is usual. Choose your answer accordingly.

Yes 68
No 69

Square stem

68 **MEADOW VETCHLING**
(Lathyrus pratensis)

(from 67)

The bright yellow, pea-like flowers of meadow vetchling are conspicuous in grassland or grassy hedgerows. They are 10–20mm long and grow in clusters of 5–12 at the extremity of each vertical flower-stalk, which is perfectly square in cross-section. Some stems may run along the ground, clinging to low vegetation with twisting tendrils. The paired leaves are narrow and pointed. Flowers May–August.

69 Is the plant a climber?

(from 67)

Answer 'Yes' if it grows by twining itself around other vegetation or clinging to it. Answer 'No' if the stem is upright and self-supporting.

Yes 70 No 71

70 **HONEYSUCKLE**
(Lonicera periclymenum)

(from 69 and 275)

Honeysuckle almost always grows by twining its rough stem around nearby bushes or trees, but will sprawl along the ground if none is available. Its fragrant flowers (4–5cm long) grow in clusters of up to a dozen, all facing outward, and attached to their stalk by long tubes. The paired leaves are oval with pointed tips and have no teeth or lobes. Honeysuckle likes shade and is found in woodland, scrub or hedgerows. Flowers June–October.

71 Do the flowers have long spurs?

(from 69)

A glance at the illustration will make it easy for you to decide on your answer.

Yes 58 No 72

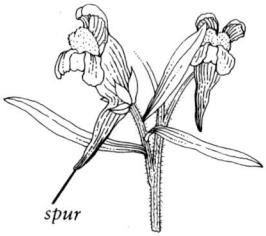

72 YELLOW RATTLE *(Rhinanthus minor)*

(from 71)

Yellow rattle almost always grows in grassland, usually in neglected meadows, sometimes in quite large patches. It may reach 60cm in height but is usually shorter (7–20cm). The two-lipped flowers, 1–1½cm long, are unusual in shape and have a conspicuous greeny-brown calyx. They grow in pairs in a loose cluster at the end of each stem, with two leaf-like bracts below each pair. The leaves are pointed and toothed. Flowers May–August.

73 How many petals has each flower?

(from 6)

Count the number of petals in each flower and choose your answer accordingly.

8–12 74
5 75
6 78
Over 12 81

74 LESSER CELANDINE
(Ranunculus ficaria)

(from 73)

The well-known lesser celandine is one of the very first flowers to blossom. Its shiny yellow flowers ($1\frac{1}{2}$–5cm) are conspicuous in March and it continues in bloom till May. The number of pointed petals may vary from 8 to 12. Each flower grows singly on its own stalk. The leaves are shiny and heart-shaped or nearly round. This plant enjoys a damp site by a stream, or on a bank beside a ditch, but also thrives in woodland or by hedgerows.

75 Do the flowers grow singly?

(from 73)

Answer 'Yes' if each flower is solitary, with its own stalk to itself. Answer 'No' if several flowers grow together in a cluster at the end of each stem.

Yes 76 No 77

Flowers single

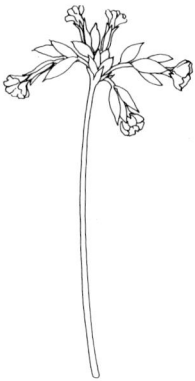

Flowers in cluster

76 PRIMROSE
(Primula vulgaris)

(from 75)

The primrose is one of the best-known and best-loved flowers. It is often the very first to appear, sometimes blooming for Christmas. The flowers (2–3cm) are pale yellow and each has its long stalk, which rises from a rosette of roughly toothed, wrinkled leaves, smooth above and slightly hairy below. The primrose grows on banks, in woodland, at roadsides and in hedgerows. Flowers till May.

77 **COWSLIP**
(Primula veris)
(from 75)

The cowslip is much the same colour as the primrose (see 76), but its flowers are smaller in diameter (8–12mm) and anything up to 30 of them (usually 8–12) dangle together from the end of each stem. The leaves are much like a primrose's, but both sides are hairy. Cowslips prefer open ground and usually grow in meadows or grazing fields. Flowers April–May.

78 Do the flowers grow singly?
(from 73)
Answer 'Yes' if each flower is solitary, with its own stalk to itself. Answer 'No' if several flowers grow together in a cluster at the end of each stem.

Yes 79 No 80

79 **WILD DAFFODIL**
(Narcissus pseudonarcissus)
(from 78)

The all-yellow wild daffodil is similar in shape to the well-known cultivated species, with its six regularly radiating petals ($3\frac{1}{2}$–5cm) and the familiar 'trumpet' in the centre. The whole plant is hairless. Long, narrow leaves rise from its base, enveloping the stem, which bears a single flower. This is a plant of grassland and woodland. Flowers February–April.

80 BOG ASPHODEL
(Narthecium ossifragum)

(from 78)

This plant, as its name indicates, is to be found only in bogland or on moors. It appears in July as a small spike of fragrant, bright yellow flowers (1–1½cm) growing at the extremity of the erect stems, with grass-like leaves rising from their bases. Blooms till September, when the flowers become more orange-coloured. (See opposite.)

81 Are the leaves hairy?

(from 73)

Answer 'Yes' if the leaves are covered in short, stiff bristly hairs. Otherwise answer 'No'.

Yes 82 No 83

82 CAT'S-EAR
(Hypochoeris radicata)

(from 81)

Cat's-ear is extremely similar to autumnal hawkbit and the same description applies (see 85), except that the flowers tend to be larger (2½–4cm) and the leaves, which are less narrow, are quite noticeably bristly. The species is found in grassland, wasteland and at roadsides. Flowers June–September.

83 Are the flowers solitary?

(from 81)

Answer 'Yes' if each flower is solitary, with its own stem to itself. Answer 'No' if each stem bears two or more flowers.

Yes 84 No 85

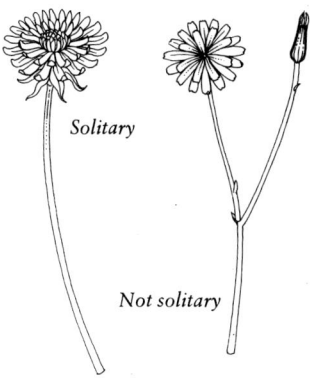

84 DANDELION
(Taraxacum officinale)

(from 83)

Almost everyone already knows the dandelion. Its large, bright yellow flowerheads (3–7cm) grow singly at the ends of thick, hollow stems. The leaves are deeply lobed and pointed. Beneath each flowerhead is a ring of bracts (like very small leaves), which at first embrace the flower but soon turn downward. This very common flower grows in open meadows or by hedgerows or roadsides. Flowers March–October.

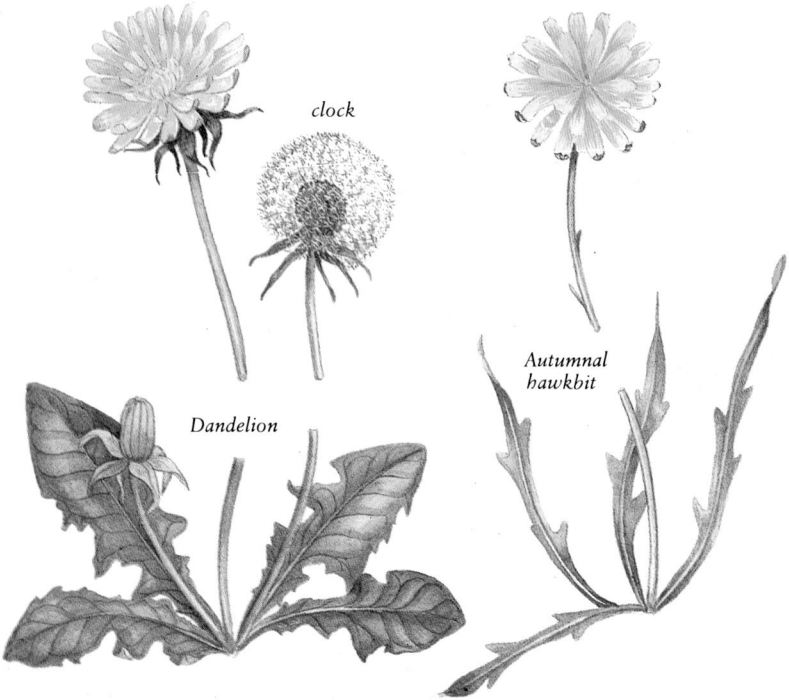

85 AUTUMNAL HAWKBIT
(Leontodon autumnalis)

(from 83)

The flowerheads are like those of a dandelion (see 84) but smaller (1–3½cm). They have fewer petal-like florets, and their undersides are often tinged with red. They grow in very loose clusters from the ends of branching stems. If the stem is cut or broken, it exudes a milky liquid. The leaves, which are narrow and lobed, are almost always hairless. Grows in grassland and wasteland. Flowers July–September.

86 COLT'S-FOOT
(Tussilago farfara)

(from 6)

Colt's-foot is specially welcome because it flowers before almost any other species. If a fine day comes in early February, clumps of it begin to appear in bloom. Until its flowers are over, no true leaves are grown. Each flowerhead grows singly, at the end of its erect stem, and looks quite like a small dandelion (1½–3cm). When the basal leaves appear, they may be very large (up to 30cm). They are toothed; and shaped something like a colt's foot, which gives the plant its name. Usually grows on wasteland and by roadsides. Flowers February–April.

87 Is the plant growing in water?

(from 1)

Answer 'Yes' if the lower part of the stem, or all the stem, is submerged in water. Answer 'No' if the plant is growing on dry land, or if only the roots are submerged.

Yes 88 No 93

88 How many petals has each flower?

(from 87)

Count the number of petals in each flower and choose your answer accordingly.

3 or 6 89
5 91
Over 10 92

89 What size are the flowers?

(from 88)

Measure the diameter of an average-sized flower to decide the right answer.

About 5mm 90
Over 20mm 285

90 CANADIAN WATERWEED
(Elodea canadensis)

(from 89 and 317)

This plant may grow in almost any water, even quite fast-moving rivers. Often the whole of it is submerged apart from any flowers and their stalks. The flowers have three petals and three rather similar sepals, which may lead beginners to think it is 6-petalled. They grow singly and are very small (5mm), regular and tinged with pink. The pointed leaves grow in close whorls of 3 around their stems. Flowers May–October.

91 THREAD-LEAVED WATER-CROWFOOT
(Ranunculus trichophyllus)

(from 88)

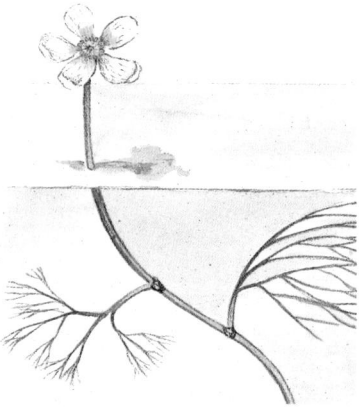

The flowers and flower-stalks of this plant are usually the only parts to appear above the water. Each flower (8–10mm) has 5 regular petals, which do not touch one another. Its centre is yellow. The few thread-like leaves are submerged. Grows in slow-moving rivers, ponds and ditches. Flowers May–June.

92 WHITE WATER-LILY
(Nymphaea alba)

(from 88)

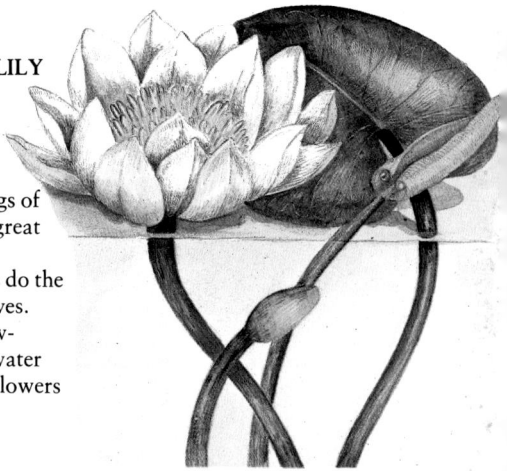

This handsome flower is quite unmistakable, with its two rings of sharply pointed petals and its great size (10–20cm). The flowers normally float on the water, as do the large, glossy, heart-shaped leaves. White water-lilies grow in slow-moving rivers, or in standing water with a depth of up to 300cm. Flowers June–September.

93 How do the leaves grow?

(from 87)

Leaves are described as being alternate, opposite, whorled or basal, depending on how they grow along their stem or stalk.

Alternate leaves grow singly, on alternating sides of the stem. Opposite leaves are in pairs, and whorled leaves in groups of 3 or more around it. Choose 'Basal only' if all the leaves grow at the very base of the plant.

The drawings should make your choice quite easy.

Alternate 94
Opposite or whorled 141
Basal only 171

Alternate *Opposite* *Whorled* *Basal only*

94 Are the flowers in umbels?

(from 93)

Flowers are said to be in umbels if they grow at the end of stalks (all much the same length) that radiate like the spokes of an umbrella from the very end of the stem.

Answer 'Yes' if the flowers are so arranged. Otherwise answer 'No'. (The small leaf-like growth at the base of some umbels is called a bract.)

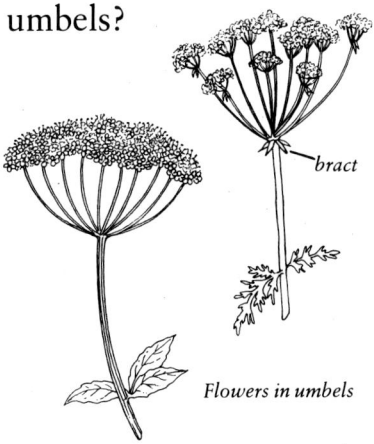

Flowers in umbels

Yes 95
No 110

95 Are the leaflets broad and undivided?

(from 94)
All flowers in this section have composite leaves, which means that each leaf is composed of several smaller leaflets. Answer 'Yes' if the leaflets are quite broad (at least one-third of their length) and, though they may be toothed or lobed, are not deeply divided. Otherwise answer 'No'.

Yes 96 No 101

96 Are the leaflets lobed?

(from 95)
Answer 'Yes' if each leaflet is quite deeply lobed. Answer 'No' if the leaflets are toothed but without lobes.

Yes 97 No 98

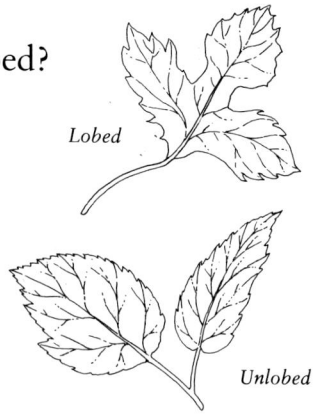

97 HOGWEED *(Heracleum sphondylium)*

(from 96)

The broad, lobed leaflets of the hogweed are quite unlike those of any other plant in this section. The whole plant is stiffly hairy. The flowers are relatively large (5–10mm) in a compound umbel (5–15cm). The hollow stem may reach a height of 200cm. Hogweed grows in woodland, along hedgerows and in grassland. Flowers June–September.

98 Is the flowerhead yellowish?

(from 96)
Answer 'Yes' if each little flower has 5 protruding yellow stamens, so that the entire flowerhead has a slight yellowish tinge. Otherwise answer 'No'.

Yes 99 No 100

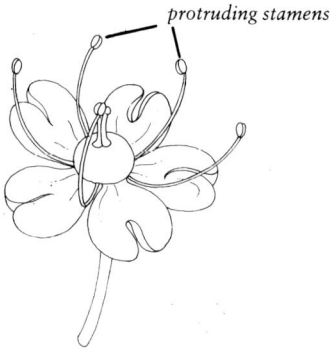

99

GOUTWEED
(Aegopodium podagraria)

(from 98)

Goutweed has very small flowers (about 1mm) with 5 notched petals. The stalks of the umbel sweep regularly upwards. They number 10–20 and each of them bears an umbel of its own, so that there may be upwards of 100 flowers to each flowerhead. Each leaf has 3–9 broad, pointed, toothed leaflets. The stem is hairless and grooved. This plant prefers shade and is usually found on wasteland or in neglected gardens, often near houses. Flowers May–June.

Hogweed

Goutweed

100

(from 98)

WILD ANGELICA
(Angelica sylvestris)

This plant prefers shade and often grows on damp ground or beside a river or lake. The umbel is composed of up to 30 stalks, which grow rather irregularly, so that the flowerhead is not flat topped. Each stalk bears an umbel of its own. The flowers (about 2mm) have 5 notched petals. Angelica, which may reach a height of 200cm, is almost completely hairless. Its large leaves have sheaths at their bases, where they embrace the stem. There are extra large leaves at the base of the plant. Flowers July–September.

101

(from 95)

Are there bracts under the umbels?

A bract looks exactly like a small leaf. Answer 'Yes' if at least one bract is growing just under each umbel. Otherwise answer 'No'.

Yes 102 No 107

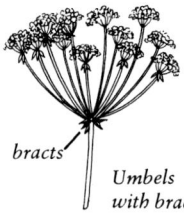

Umbels with bracts

Umbels without bracts

102

(from 101)

Are the bracts conspicuous?

Answer 'Yes' if the bracts are large and unmistakable. Answer 'No' if they are so small that you might nearly miss them.

Yes 103 No 104

103 **WILD CARROT**
(Daucus carota)

(from 102)

The flowerhead of wild carrot is a compound umbel, which means that each main umbel is itself composed of many secondary umbels. The central flower of each of the secondary umbels is usually tinged with pink. There are very conspicuous, deeply-divided bracts, which look like leaves, immediately under each main umbel. The leaves, also deeply divided, are sheathed where they meet the erect, stiffly hairy stem. This plant often grows by the sea-shore, or in grassy places anywhere. Flowers June to August.

104 Is the stem covered with purple spots?

(from 102)

Answer 'Yes' if the stem is quite liberally covered with purple spots or blotches (see illustration to 105).

Answer 'No' if there is no such purple colouring.

Yes 105 No 106

105 **HEMLOCK**
(Conium maculatum)

(from 104)

This extremely poisonous plant may grow to a great height (200–300cm) and develops a very thick, hollow stem. The entire plant is hairless. The flowers grow in a compound umbel, meaning that each main umbel is itself composed of secondary umbels. The individual flowers are small (2mm) and have 5 petals. The bracts beneath each main umbel are also small. The leaves are compound and fern-like. Hemlock often grows quite near water or on damp ground, usually wasteland. Flowers June–July.

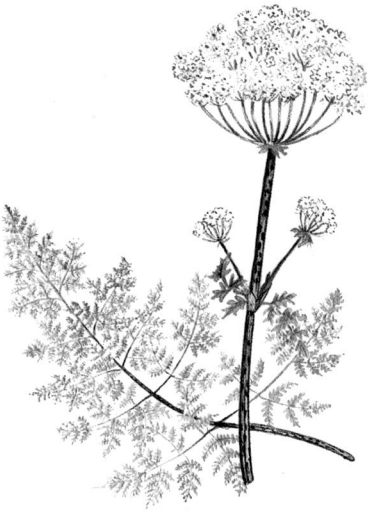

106 **UPRIGHT HEDGE-PARSLEY**
(Torilis japonica)

(from 104)

This plant grows to a height of 50–100cm. It has a slender, erect stem. The umbels are quite small, with 5–12 main flower-stalks. There are small bracts under each main umbel. The flowers are tinged with purple. Each leaf is composed of several deeply divided leaflets, which grow in pairs along their stalks. The whole plant is hairy. It usually grows on roadsides, but also occurs in wasteland or by hedgerows. Flowers July–September.

107 When does it flower?

(from 101)

Of the two most likely remaining species, one blooms from April till mid-June; the other does not come out till late June or early July. Choose your answer accordingly.

April–June 108
July–August 109

108 **COW PARSLEY**
(Anthriscus sylvestris)

(from 107)

This is probably the commonest of all the plants with umbels and it is the first of them to come out, usually in April. The flowers are relatively large (2–4mm) and somewhat irregular in shape. The umbels are 2–6cm in diameter. The compound leaves are very deeply divided. The stem of cow parsley is erect and grooved, and reaches a height of over 100cm. Usually grows on roadsides or in hedgerows. Flowers April–June.

109

BURNET-SAXIFRAGE
(Pimpinella saxifraga)

(from 107)

Rather similar to cow parsley (see 108) apart from its later flowering. The 5-petalled flowers tend to be more regular and smaller (2mm). They are again in compound umbels, 2–5cm in diameter. All the leaves are compound. The leaflets of those on the stem are very deeply divided, but those at the base of the plant are broader. The ridged, erect stems have rough hairs and grow up to 100cm high. Found in dry grassland. Flowers July–August.

110

Are the flowers bell-shaped?

(from 94)
Answer 'Yes' if the petals are fused together so that they cannot easily be distinguished, and the flowers are shaped more or less like a bell or funnel. Answer 'No' if each petal is clearly distinct down to its base.

Yes 111 No 115

Bell-shaped

Funnel-shaped

111

Is the plant a climber?

(from 110)
Answer 'Yes' if it grows by twining itself around other vegetation. Answer 'No' if the stem is upright and self-supporting.

Yes 112 No 114

112

How big are the flowers?

(from 111)
Measure the diameter of an average-sized flower to decide on the answer.

2cm 212
3½–7cm 113

113 HEDGE BINDWEED
(Calystegia sepium)

(from 112)

The bindweeds are at once distinguished, with their twisty stems twining strongly round nearby vegetation. The flowers of the hedge bindweed (3½–7cm) are pure white, with no distinct petals. They grow singly on quite long stalks. The whole plant is hairless. The glossy, dark green leaves are shaped like arrowheads. Grows in hedgerows and woodland margins. Flowers July–September.

114 COMMON COMFREY
(Symphytum officinale)

(from 111, 209 and 303)

The flowers of the comfrey may be bluish-purple, pink or white, but the fully-opened flowers on one plant are always the same colour. They usually hang downwards, growing in small clusters at the end of the branched stems. The whole plant is noticeably hairy. The leaves are quite long and narrow, and grow alternately. Comfrey likes damp places and is often found growing by rivers and streams. Flowers May–June.

115 How many petals has each flower?

(from 110)

Count the number of petals, or petal-like sepals, in each flower and choose your answer accordingly.

4 116
5 120
6 or more 134

116 What size are the flowers?

(from 115)

Measure the diameter of an average-sized flower and choose your answer accordingly.

25–40mm 117
12–18mm 310
6mm 118
2½mm 119

lilac form

117 WILD RADISH *(Raphanus raphanistrum)*

(from 116, 20 and 308)

The flowers of wild radish may be white, yellow or lilac, often with darker veins, but the flowers of any given specimen are always the same colour. The 4 petals are entirely separate and do not touch each other. The flowers are in loose clusters and the lower ones develop into long, upright seed-pods while the upper ones are still in flower. The upper leaves are toothed and sometimes lobed. This is a common weed of arable land. Flowers May–September.

118 GARLIC MUSTARD
(Alliaria petiolata)

(from 116)

The large, glossy leaves of garlic mustard have long stems and are strongly toothed. The flowers are in clusters and quite small (6mm) in relation to the plant's height (up to 120cm). The stem is straight and unbranched. Garlic mustard is virtually hairless and smells of garlic when crushed. It often grows beside walls, on the edge of woodland or in hedgerows. Flowers April–June.

119 SHEPHERD'S-PURSE
(Capsella bursa-pastoris)

(from 116)

This is one of the commonest flowers and is in bloom for nearly all the year. Its very small flowers (2–3mm) are regular and grow in clusters. They develop into heart-shaped seed-pods. Most of the leaves are at the base of the plant, and are usually deeply divided. The upper leaves, which embrace the stem, are neither divided nor toothed. Shepherd's-purse grows almost anywhere, but is very often found on wasteland or on roadsides.

120 Is the stem thorny?

(from 115)

Answer 'Yes' if the stem and stalks have sharp thorns or spines. Answer 'No' if they are completely thornless.

Yes 121 No 123

121 Are the petals heart-shaped?

(from 120)

Answer 'Yes' if each petal has an indentation, making it appear heart-shaped. Otherwise answer 'No'.

Yes 122 No 229

122 BURNET ROSE *(Rosa pimpinellifolia)*

(from 121)

The petals of the burnet rose are pure white or creamy white without any pink or red. The flowers (2–4cm) are regular, with bright yellow stamens in their centre. The compound leaves have 5 or more narrow, toothed leaflets, arranged in pairs. The stem and stalks are thickly covered in sharp spines and thorns. This rose most often grows by the sea on sandy, grassy land, but also appears inland, on downs, heaths and scrubland. Flowers May–June.

123 Is the plant a climber?

(from 120)

Answer 'Yes' if it grows by twining round other vegetation. Answer 'No' if the stem is upright and self-supporting.

Yes 124 No 126

124 Are the leaves 5-lobed?

(from 123)

Answer 'Yes' if each leaf is divided into 5 lobes like the fingers of your hand. Otherwise answer 'No'.

Yes 362 No 125

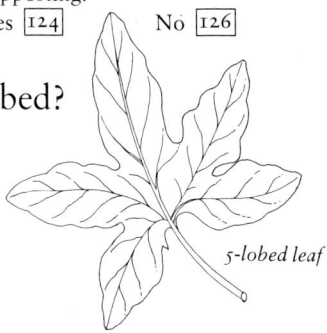

5-lobed leaf

125

(from 124 and 246)

BLACK BINDWEED
(Fallopia convolvulus)

The twining black bindweed has very small greenish-white or pinkish flowers, which grow in little clusters on stalks rising from the leaf-axils (where the leaf-stalks join the stem). The leaves are dark green, hairless and glossy, with powdery white undersides. They are shaped like spearheads. The stem may reach a length of over 100cm. The plant often grows on wasteland or in hedgerows. Flowers July–October.

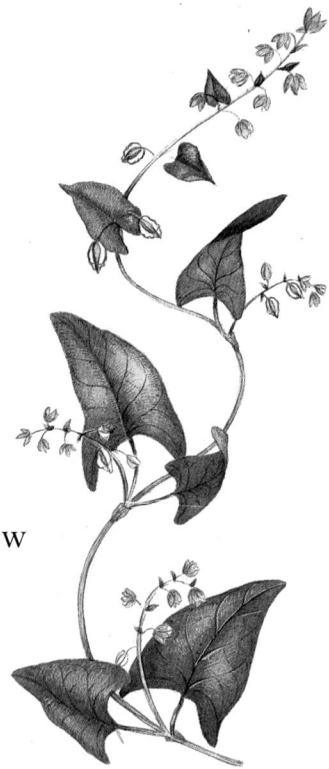

126

(from 123)

Do the flowers grow in large clusters?

Answer 'Yes' if each flowerhead is a large, compact cluster of many small flowers. Answer 'No' if the flowers grow in little groups of 1–6.

Yes 127

No 130

Flowers in large cluster

Flowers in little groups

127 Do the leaves have broad segments?

(from 126)

Answer 'Yes' if the divisions of each leaf are broad and flat. Answer 'No' if they are thin and fern-like.

Yes 128 No 129

Broad flat leaflets

Thin fern-like leaflets

128 MEADOWSWEET *(Filipendula ulmaria)*

(from 127)

This plant prefers damp ground, and is most common in old meadowland, in pasture or by rivers. It is very conspicuous, reaching a height of over 100cm with large, dense clusters of creamy-white flowers which have a distinctive bittersweet smell. The stems and stalks are often reddish. The compound leaves have 5 or more strongly toothed leaflets. Flowers June–September.

129 YARROW *(Achillea millefolium)*

(from 127)

The yarrow's flowers (4–6mm) grow in smooth, flat-topped flowerheads, whose stalks do not all radiate from exactly the same point on the stem.

Meadowsweet

The erect stem is covered with soft hairs. All the leaves are very deeply divided and fern-like. Yarrow is to be found in grassland or wasteland, and grows in hedgerows and by roadsides. Flowers June–August.

130 Are the leaves straight and narrow?

(from 126)

Answer 'Yes' if the short leaves are narrow and straight-sided. Answer 'No' if they are lobed or composite.

Yes 131 No 132

Narrow leaf

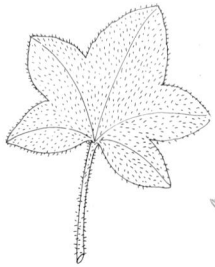

Lobed leaf

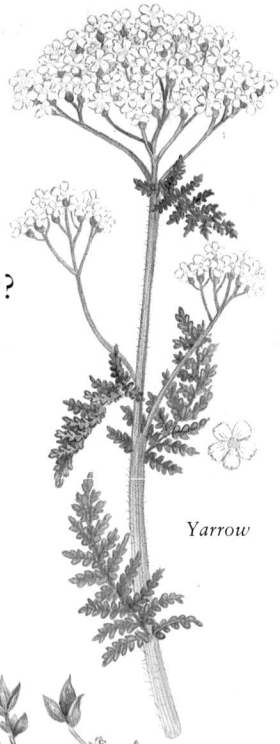

Yarrow

131 KNOTGRASS *(Polygonum aviculare)*

(from 130)

Knotgrass usually grows prostrate but is sometimes erect and may reach a height of 200cm. It has very small regular flowers in the axils of the leaves (the points where they join the stem). The leaves are stalkless, narrow and quite pointed. Knotgrass often grows by the seashore, or on wasteland or farmland. Flowers July–October.

132 How big are the flowers?

(from 130)

Measure the diameter of an average-sized flower and choose your answer accordingly.

4–6mm 133
10–20mm 177

133 RUE-LEAVED SAXIFRAGE *(Saxifraga tridactylites)*

(from 132)

This small plant, not usually more than 10cm high, has regular flowers (4–6mm) which grow in very loose clusters, each with a stalk of its own. Its lower leaves are quite large and deeply lobed, whilst those higher up the stem are smaller and undivided. The leaves and the stem, which is covered with sticky hairs, may be strongly tinged with red. The plant usually grows on walls or on sandy ground. Flowers April–June.

134 Are the flowers daisy-like?

(from 115)

Answer 'Yes' if the flowers look like large daisies, with white rays and a yellow centre. Otherwise answer 'No'.

Yes 135 No 138

135 Are the leaves very narrow?

(from 134)

Answer 'Yes' if all the leaves are divided into extremely narrow segments, little wider than threads. Answer 'No' if they are quite broad, despite being deeply lobed.

Yes 136 No 137

Very narrow leaf

Quite broad leaf

136 SCENTLESS MAYWEED
(Tripleurospermum inodorum)

(from 135)

Easily distinguished from the more common ox-eye daisy by its extremely narrow leaves, scentless mayweed is usually found as a weed of cultivated and waste ground. The flowers (1½–5cm) are solitary, each with its own long stalk. There is usually a leaf where the flower-stalk joins the stem. The whole plant is hairless. Flowers June–September.

Scentless mayweed

Ox-eye daisy

137 OX-EYE DAISY
(Leucanthemum vulgare)

(from 135)

The ox-eye daisy's leaves are much broader than the scentless mayweed's. They are deeply lobed, dark green and stalkless. The whole plant is almost hairless. This well-known, easily recognizable flower grows in grassland or wasteland and blooms June–August.

138 Is it a climber?

(from 134)
Answer 'Yes' if the plant grows by twining itself around other vegetation. Answer 'No' if the stem is upright and self-supporting.

Yes 139 No 140

Black bryony

139 BLACK BRYONY *(Tamus communis)*

(from 138 and 357)

The stem of black bryony twists firmly around the supporting vegetation. Its heart-shaped leaves are glossy and have quite long stalks. The flowers are small (4–5mm) and grow in little clusters where the leaf-stalks join the stem. Although they appear to have six petals, three of them are in fact sepals. Black bryony grows in hedgerows, by woodland margins and in scrubland. Flowers May–July.

140 GREATER BUTTERFLY ORCHID *(Platanthera chlorantha)*

(from 138)

The flowers of this orchid (18–23mm) are arranged in a loose spike. They are white, tinged with green, and very fragrant. There are two large, pointed leaves at the base of the plant, and smaller ones growing alternately along the erect stem. The whole plant is hairless. This orchid likes chalky ground and usually grows in woods and grassland. Flowers May–June.

(Note: the common spotted orchid

usually has pinkish flowers but sometimes they are white tinged with pink or occasionally pure white. If the above description does not seem correct, have a look at the spotted orchid – see 253.)

141 Are the flowers regular?

(from 93)
Answer 'Yes' if all the petals of each flower are equal in size and the same shape. Otherwise answer 'No'.

Yes 142 No 166

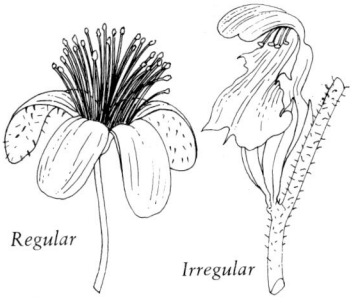

142 How many petals has each flower?

(from 141)
Count the number of petals (or petal-like sepals) in each flower and choose your answer accordingly.

4 143
5 147
6–7 146

143 Are the leaves opposite or whorled?

(from 142)
Decide whether the leaves grow in opposing pairs along the stem, or whether they are in whorls around it.

Opposite 144
Whorled 145

144 TRAVELLER'S-JOY *(Clematis vitalba)*

(from 143)

The flowers (2cm) grow in a loose cluster on a stalk which arises from the point where the leaf-stalk joins the stem. The leaves are composite: each one has 3–5 pointed, usually toothed, leaflets growing in opposite pairs. The plant twines around the surrounding vegetation for support. It grows on the edges of woods, in hedgerows and scrubland. Flowers July–August. (See opposite.)

145 GOOSEGRASS
(Galium aparine)

(from 143)

This plant, also known as cleavers, is a favourite in children's games because it sticks to clothes and hair with the tiny spines on its stems and fruits. It has extremely small flowers (2mm) in loose clusters on short stalks. Its very narrow leaves grow in whorls around its square stem. Sometimes it grows erect, but more often sprawls over nearby vegetation. Often found on wasteland, in hedgerows or on roadsides. Flowers June–August.

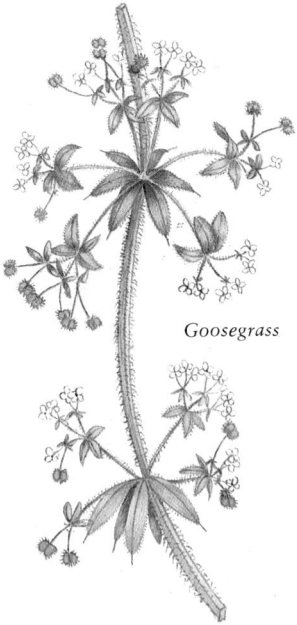

Goosegrass

146 WOOD ANEMONE
(Anemone nemorosa)

(from 142)

This is one of the first flowers to open in the springtime. Its solitary blooms (2–4cm) have 6–7 pure white sepals (which look exactly like petals). There is a whorl of deeply-divided leaves halfway up the stem. The whole plant is hairless. It is usually found in deciduous woodland. Flowers March–May.

Traveller's-joy

Wood anemone

147 Are the petals indented?

(from 142)

Answer 'Yes' if there is a clear indentation in each petal, so that it is either heart-shaped or deeply divided. Answer 'No' if the petals are rounded or pointed, without any such indentation.

Yes 148 No 159

Petals indented

Petals not indented

148 Does it have a square stem?

(from 147)

Answer 'Yes' if the stem is noticeably square-shaped in cross-section. Answer 'No' if it is rounded.

Yes 149 No 152

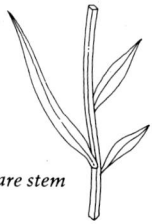

Square stem

149 How big are the flowers?

(from 148)

Measure the diameter of an average-sized flower and decide your answer accordingly.

5–12mm 150
Over 15mm 151

150 LESSER STITCHWORT *(Stellaria graminea)*

(from 149)

The small flowers (5–12mm) have deeply divided petals. They grow on individual stalks, which rise from the points where the leaves join the stem. The stalkless leaves are small, narrow and pointed. Grows in grassland or woodland. Flowers May–August. (See opposite.)

151 GREATER STITCHWORT
(Stellaria holostea)

(from 149)

Similar to lesser stitchwort (see 150) but the flowers are larger (2–3cm) as are the leaves. It is found in much the same places, but tends to flower sooner, in April–June.

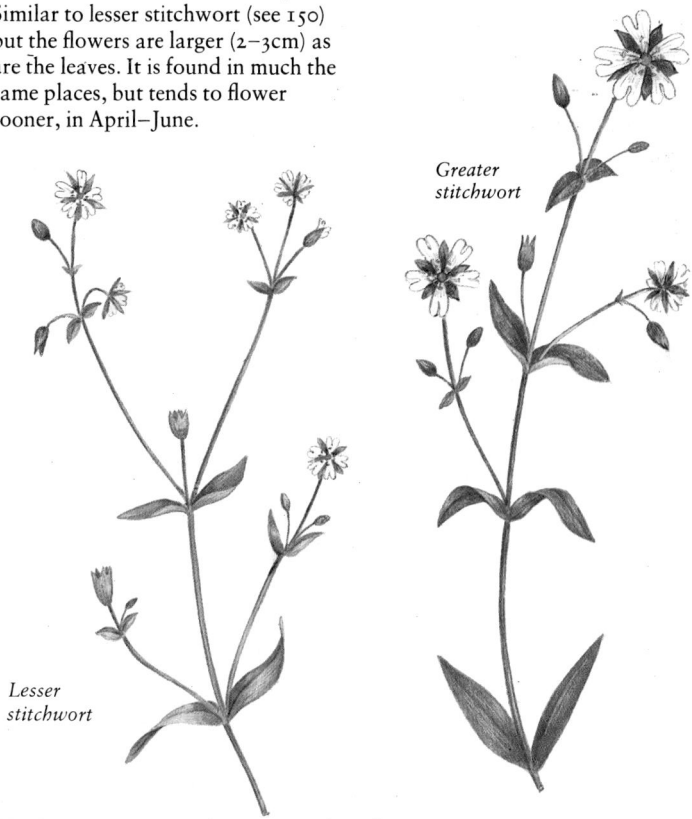

152 How big are the flowers?

(from 148)

Measure the diameter of an average-sized flower and decide your answer accordingly.

Up to 15mm 153
Over 18mm 156

153 Is the plant noticeably hairy?

(from 152)

Answer 'Yes' if the stem and leaves are noticeably hairy. Answer 'No' if they are hairless or nearly so.

Yes 154 No 155

154 **COMMON MOUSE-EAR**
(Cerastium fontanum)

(from 153)

The leaves and stem of this common little plant are noticeably hairy. There is a pointed green sepal between each of the 5 deeply-notched petals in each flower. The flowers (10–15mm) grow in loose clusters. All the leaves are stalkless. Common mouse-ear may grow almost anywhere and flowers April–September.

155 **CHICKWEED**
(Stellaria media)

(from 153)

This plant has a weak stem and tends to sprawl over the ground. The flowers (8–10mm) have petals that are very deeply divided. There are prominent pointed sepals between the petals. The leaves are oval and pointed; the upper ones are stalkless but some of those at the base of the plant may have stalks. Chickweed is very common in gardens, fields and wasteland. Flowers all year.

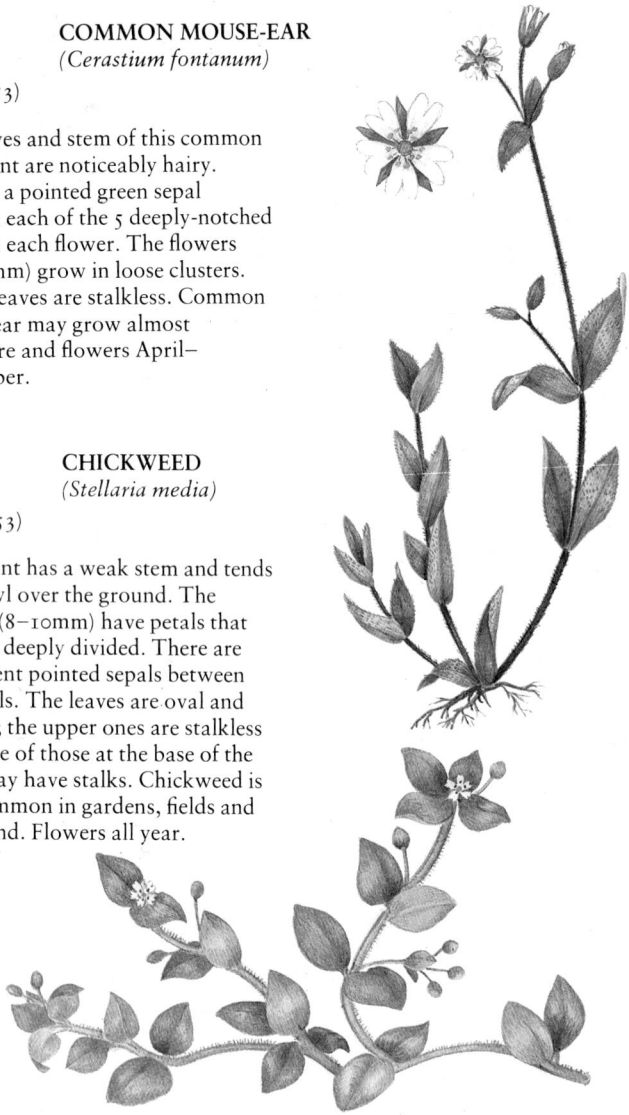

156 Is the plant noticeably hairy?

(from 152)

Answer 'Yes' if the stem and leaves are noticeably hairy. Answer 'No' if they are almost or completely hairless, except perhaps for some light down.

Yes 157 No 158

157 **WHITE CAMPION**
(Silene alba)
(from 156)

The stem of white campion is usually branched and may reach almost 100cm in height. The few flowers ($2\frac{1}{2}$–3cm) have deeply notched petals and grow in small loose clusters. They usually open in the evenings. There is a prominent, green or brown calyx-tube under each flower. The pointed leaves are stalkless, except perhaps towards the base. This is quite a common weed of arable land and also grows in hedgerows and on wasteland. Flowers May–September.

158 **BLADDER CAMPION**
(Silene vulgaris)
(from 156)

This plant is very similar to white campion (see 157), but the flowers are smaller (15mm) and the swollen calyx-tube beneath each of them is even more conspicuous. It is found in much the same places but has a shorter flowering season, July–August.

159 Do the leaves grow in whorls?
(from 147)

Answer 'Yes' if the leaves are very narrow and grow in whorls along the stem. Answer 'No' if they are not noticeably narrow and grow along the stem in opposite pairs.

Yes 160 No 161

White campion

Bladder campion

160

(from 159)

CORN SPURREY
(Spergula arvensis)

The very small white flowers (4–7mm) grow in loose clusters at the end of the stems, which are branched and grow rather weakly. The leaves are very unusual, being arranged in whorls and needle-like. The whole plant is usually sticky. Most often seen in cornfields or on wasteland; prefers sandy soil. Flowers June–August.

161

(from 159)

Are the leaves hairy?

Answer 'Yes' if the leaves are noticeably covered in hairs. Answer 'No' if they are completely or nearly hairless.

Yes 162 No 163

162

(from 161)

THYME-LEAVED SANDWORT
(Arenaria serpyllifolia)

This plant is distinguished by its very small, stalkless leaves, and by its small flowers (5–6mm). The conspicuous pointed sepals are rather longer than the petals and alternate between them. There are 1–2 flowers on individual stalks towards the ends of the branching stems. Thyme-leaved sandwort often grows on walls and is also found in grassland, on arable ground and on wasteland. Flowers June–August.

163 Is it growing at the seaside?

(from 161)
Answer 'Yes' if the plant is growing on or near a seaside beach or coastal sand dunes. Otherwise answer 'No'.

Yes 164 No 165

164 SEA SANDWORT *(Honkenya peploides)*

(from 163)

This plant almost always grows by the sea, where it may be found creeping among stones and shingle or in sand. It is completely hairless with rather fleshy, pointed, stalkless leaves. The flowers are similar to those of thyme-leaved sandwort (see 162) but rather larger (6–10mm). They are solitary, growing on short stalks from the ends of the stem, or from the points on the stem where pairs of leaves grow. Flowers May–August.

165 FAIRY FLAX *(Linum catharticum)*

(from 163)

This plant is distinguished by its very small flowers and leaves. The flowers (4–6mm) grow singly, each at the end of its own stalk. The paired, oval leaves are pointed, hairless and stalkless. Fairy flax, also known as purging flax, is found on grassland and heaths. It flowers June–September.

166 Are the leaves more than 10mm long?

(from 141)
Measure the length of an average leaf and choose your answer accordingly.

Yes 167 No 170

167 Does each flower have two divided petals?

(from 166)

Answer 'Yes' if the flowers are very small and have only two petals each, deeply divided so that there may appear to be 4. Otherwise answer 'No'.

Yes 168 No 169

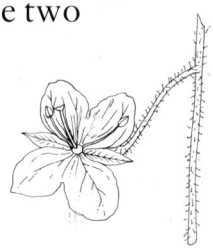

2 divided petals

Enchanter's-nightshade

168 ENCHANTER'S-NIGHTSHADE
(Circaea lutetiana)

(from 167)

The very small flowers (4–8mm) grow in a loose spike. The plant is erect and the stem slightly hairy. The oval, pointed leaves are in opposite pairs; they have shallow teeth and are stalked. Enchanter's-nightshade is found in woods or hedgerows. Flowers June–August.

White dead-nettle

169 WHITE DEAD-NETTLE
(Lamium album)

(from 167)

White dead-nettle looks like a common stinging nettle, except for its pure white flowers, which grow in well-spaced whorls around its hairy stem. The toothed leaves are long and pointed. It may be found on wasteground, in hedgerows or by roadsides. Flowers April–October.

170

COMMON EYEBRIGHT
(Euphrasia nemorosa)

(from 166)

This is a small plant, seldom more than 20cm in height, with a branched stem. The flowers are mainly white, but tinged with yellow and purple. The small leaves are stalkless and regularly toothed. Eyebright grows in grassy places and flowers May–September.

171

Do the flowers grow singly?

(from 93)

Answer 'Yes' if each flower is solitary, with its own stalk or stem to itself. Answer 'No' if several or many flowers grow close together; the flower-stalks, if any, are very short.

(Note: the well-known clovers may at first appear to have flowers growing singly, but in fact each flowerhead is composed of many tiny flowers and you should answer 'No'.)

Yes 172 No 184

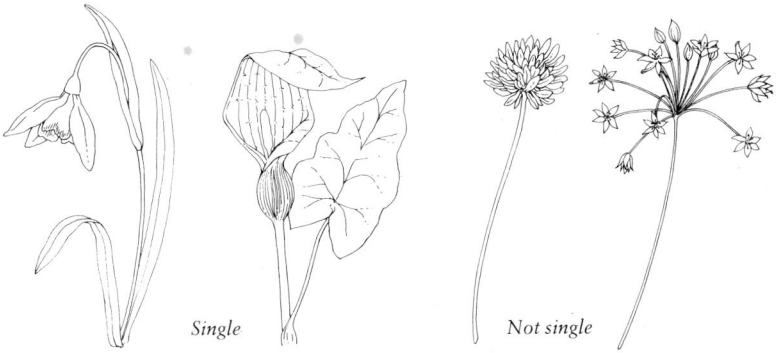

172

Are the flowers regular?

(from 171)

Answer 'Yes' if all the petals of each flower are equal in size and the same shape. Otherwise answer 'No'.

Yes 173 No 183

173 How many petals has each flower?

(from 172)
Count the number of petals in each flower and choose your answer accordingly.

3 or 6 174
5 175
Over 6 182

174 SNOWDROP *(Galanthus nivalis)*

(from 173)

The snowdrop is widely planted and only occasionally grows wild. It is specially welcome because it is one of the very first plants to appear in bloom in the early days of the year. The solitary, nodding flowers (14–17mm) seem to have 6 petals – 3 larger ones in an outside ring and 3 smaller ones inside them – but the former are in fact sepals. The hairless leaves are long and narrow. Snowdrops grow in woodland and in hedgerows. They flower January–March.

175 Are the leaves in the form of trefoils?

(from 173)
Answer 'Yes' if each leaf is divided into 3 equal leaflets like a clover's. Such leaves are called trefoils. Answer 'No' if the leaves are simple and undivided.

Yes 176 No 181

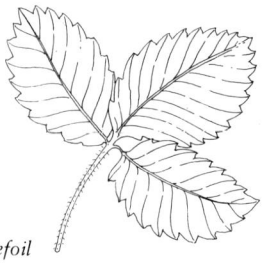

Trefoil

Simple leaf

176 Are the leaflets toothed?

(from 175)
Examine the edges of the leaflets and answer 'Yes' if they are quite clearly toothed. Answer 'No' if they are smooth and toothless.

Yes 177 No 180

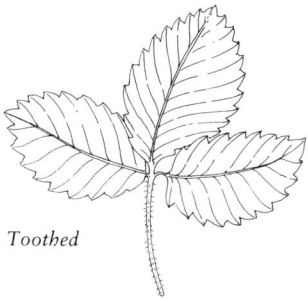

Toothed

Untoothed

177 Are the petals rounded?

(from 176 and 132)
Answer 'Yes' if the petals of each flower are unmistakably rounded. Answer 'No' if they have a small indentation so that they are heart-shaped.

Yes 178 No 179

Rounded

Heart-shaped

178 WILD STRAWBERRY 6/12

(Fragaria vesca)

(from 177) Grassmere, Cumbria

The wild strawberry is best known for its delicious fruit, which resembles the well-known garden varieties but is very much smaller (less than 10mm). The flowers (12–18mm) are perfectly regular. It is usually found on shady banks, woodland edges and hedgerows. Flowers May–June.

179

BARREN STRAWBERRY
(Potentilla sterilis)

(from 177)

This plant is almost identical to the wild strawberry (see 178) except for the shape of its petals and its failure to bear conspicuous fruit. It flowers sooner, from March to June.

180

WOOD-SORREL
(Oxalis acetosella)

(from 176)

The wood-sorrel's leaves grow singly on the ends of long stalks, which rise from the base of the plant. The 3 equal leaflets making up each leaf are noticeably indented so that they are heart-shaped. The flowers (10–25mm), which also grow singly, are perfectly regular and usually drooping. The whole plant is hairless. Wood-sorrel almost always grows in deciduous woodland. Flowers April–May.

181

GRASS-OF-PARNASSUS
(Parnassia palustris)

(from 175)

This plant of the fens and marshes has erect stems bearing single flowers ($1\frac{1}{2}$–3cm), which are white with yellow centres. The heart-shaped, hairless leaves are also single, each with its own long stalk, rising from the base. There is also, usually, a single stalkless leaf, less than half-way up the flower-stem. Flowers July–October.

182

(from 173)

DAISY
(Bellis perennis)

The daisy is perhaps the best-known of all wild flowers. Its small white flowers (1½–3cm), yellow-centred and tipped with scarlet, grow singly on delicate stems. The short-stalked leaves are bluntly toothed, and, like the stems, they are hairy. Daisies grow on lawns and grassland. They flower March–October.

183

(from 172)

LORDS-AND-LADIES
(Arum maculatum)

This plant is immediately recognizable because of its extremely unusual flowerhead. The true flowers are very small and hidden at the base of the poker-like flower-spike, surrounded by the conspicuous, greenish-white flower-hood, which is erect, pointed and 15–25cm in length. The shiny, hairless leaves grow on long stalks from the base. Lords-and-ladies, also known as cuckoo-pint, grows in woods and hedgerows. Flowers April–May.

184

(from 171)

Does it have rounded flowerheads?

Answer 'Yes' if the plant is a clover, with many very small flowers growing close together in a rounded flowerhead. Otherwise answer 'No'.

Yes 185

No 186

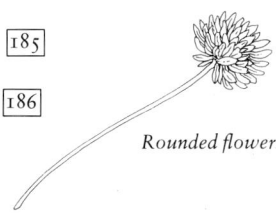

Rounded flowerhead

185 **WHITE CLOVER**
(Trifolium repens)

(from 184)

This well-known little flower is completely hairless. The leaves are very regular trefoils, each composed of 3 rounded, indented leaflets. The flowerheads grow from long, leafless stalks; they turn brown from the bases upward. White clover puts out a long, creeping stem, which may take root at intervals. It is found on lawns and grassland. Flowers June–September.

186 Are the leaves sticky?

(from 184)
Answer 'Yes' if the leaves are fringed with long red sticky glands.
Otherwise answer 'No'.

Yes 187 No 188

187 **ROUND-LEAVED SUNDEW**
(Drosera rotundifolia)

(from 186)

This little plant's most conspicuous feature is its small, round, fleshy leaves, which are covered in red glands. They grow on individual stalks. The tiny flowers are in a long spike at the end of each flower-stalk. They are perfectly regular with 5–6 pointed white petals, alternating with the same number of noticeable green sepals. This is a plant of moorland, marsh and bogland. It flowers June–August.

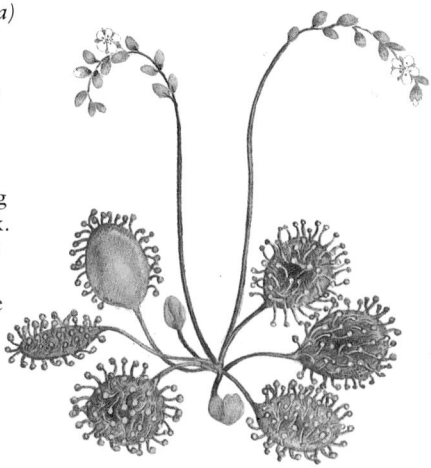

188 Are the leaves toothed?

(from 186)
Answer 'Yes' if the leaves are toothed all round their margin. Answer 'No' if they are quite smooth.

Yes 290 No 189

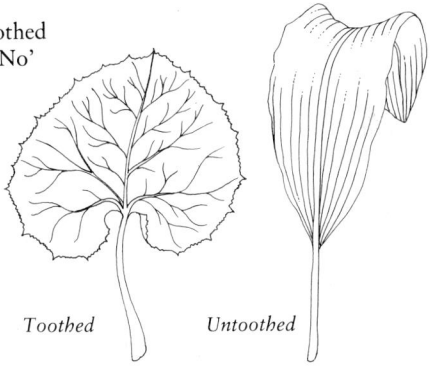

189 Are the flowers sweet-smelling?

(from 188)
Answer 'Yes' if they are noticeably sweet-scented. Answer 'No' if the whole plant smells strongly of garlic.

Yes 190 No 191

190 LILY-OF-THE-VALLEY
(Convallaria majalis)

(from 189)

This plant is more often cultivated in gardens, but also grows truly wild in dry woodland. Each stem bears a long cluster of 6–12 pure white, drooping, bell-shaped flowers, all facing the same way. The pointed leaves, which are stalked and hairless, grow in pairs at the base of each stem. Flowers May–June.

flower

berry

191 **RAMSONS**
(Allium ursinum)
(from 189)

The star-like, pure white flowers grow singly on short radiating stalks at the end of each stem. The broad, pointed leaves are on individual stalks, arising from the base of the plant, which has a strong smell of garlic. It grows in woods and hedgerows. Flowers April–June.

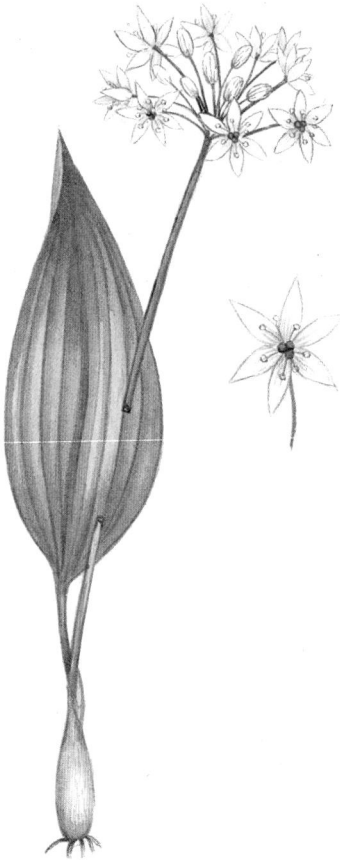

192 (from 1)

How do the leaves grow?

Leaves are described as being alternate, opposite, whorled or basal, depending on how they grow along their stem or stalk.

Alternate leaves grow singly, on alternating sides of the stalk. Opposite leaves are in pairs, and whorled leaves in groups of 3 or more around it. Choose 'Basal only' if all the leaves grow at the very base of the plant.

The drawings should make your choice quite easy.

Alternate 193
Opposite or whorled 255
Basal only 281

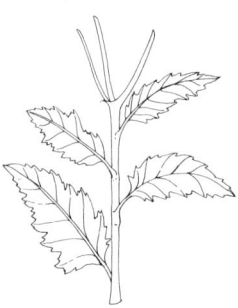

Alternate

Opposite

Whorled

Basal only

193 Are the flowers thistle-like?

(from 192)
Ignore the leaves and stem (which may or may not be prickly) and examine one of the flowerheads. Answer 'Yes' if it has the well-known appearance of a member of the thistle family, with no obvious petals but a mass of purple florets (see illustration) which grow upwards, very close together, from a more or less rounded base. This base is known as the involucre. Answer 'No' in all other cases.

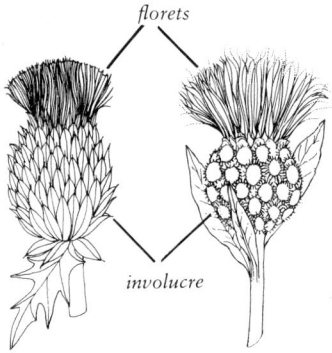

Thistle-like flowers

Yes 194 No 205

194 Are the leaves prickly?

(from 193)
This question needs no elaboration. Yes 195 No 202

195 Is the stem spiny?

(from 194)
Answer 'Yes' if the upright stem of the plant is covered with sharp spines or prickles for all or almost all its length. Answer 'No' if it is spineless.

Yes 196 No 201

196 Is the involucre very sharp and spiny?

(from 195)
The involucre is the lower part of the flowerhead, from which the florets grow upward. Answer 'Yes' if it is large and covered with long, sharp spines. Otherwise answer 'No'.

Yes 197 No 198

Involucre sharp and spiny

197 **SPEAR THISTLE**
(Cirsium vulgare)
(from 196)

Spear thistle is best distinguished by its extra large, very spiny involucre (see 196). It grows taller than most other thistles, up to 150cm, and its leaves and stems are also extremely spiny. The undersides of the leaves, which are deeply lobed and pointed, are often whitish with soft hairs. The flowerheads either grow singly or in small open clusters of 2–5. Spear thistles grow in grassland, wasteland or on roadsides. They flower July–October.

Spear thistle

198 Do the flowerheads grow in tight clusters?
(from 196)

Answer 'Yes' if most of the flowerheads grow in quite a tight cluster at the top of the stem. Answer 'No' if they are in an open cluster of 3–5 flowerheads, each with its own noticeable stalk.

Yes 199 No 200

199 **MARSH THISTLE**
(Cirsium palustre)
(from 198)

As its name implies, this very prickly thistle prefers a damp site, but it also grows in quite dry fields, hedgerows and woodland. It has relatively small flowerheads (1–1½cm), growing in close clusters at the top of the stem or stalks. The narrow leaves are lobed and spiny; except at the base of the plant they are stalkless. Flowers July–September.

Marsh thistle

200 **WELTED THISTLE**
(Carduus acanthoides)
(from 198)

This thistle is distinguished by the very fine white hairs on the undersides of its leaves and on its stem. It has quite large flowerheads ($1\frac{1}{2}$–$2\frac{1}{2}$cm). Their involucres (see 196) are covered with many pointed bracts but they are not spiny. The leaves are deeply lobed, stalkless and very prickly. This plant grows in wasteland, open woodland, hedgerows or often near water. Flowers June–August.

Welted thistle

Creeping thistle

201 **CREEPING THISTLE**
(Cirsium arvense)
(from 195)

Creeping thistles spread rapidly and often form a dense patch in open grassland or wasteland. They send up many erect, branching stems, which end in open clusters of small, light purple flowerheads. The lobed leaves are less prickly than those of other common thistles; the upper ones are stalkless and embrace the stems. Flowers July–September.

202 Are the leaves narrow?

(from 194)
Answer 'Yes' if the leaves are at least three times as long as they are broad. Otherwise answer 'No'.

Yes 203 No 204

203 COMMON KNAPWEED
(Centaurea nigra)

(from 202)

Common knapweeds look like thistles without the prickles. They have branching, erect stems, with a single purple flowerhead at the end of every branch. The many purple florets arise from a spherical, dark brown involucre (see 196). The leaves are very narrow and pointed, with occasional lobes. Usually found on roadsides or in grassland. Flowers June–September.

204 LESSER BURDOCK
(Arctium minus)

(from 202)

The flowerheads resemble those of a thistle, but the plant is at once distinguished by its very broad smooth leaves. They grow at intervals on stalks from the erect, reddish-coloured stem. The flowerheads grow from short stalks in open clusters. Lesser burdock may reach a height of 150cm, when it becomes quite bushy in appearance, with very large leaves (up to 40cm long) towards the base. Flowers July–September.

205 Does it have rounded flowerheads?

(from 193)
Answer 'Yes' if the plant is a clover, with many small flowers in a compact, rounded flowerhead. Otherwise answer 'No'.

Yes 206 No 207

206

RED CLOVER
(Trifolium pratense)

(from 205)

There is usually a flowerhead at the end of every stem, with a small pair of stalkless leaves immediately below it. The main leaves are stalked; each is composed of 3 separate leaflets, forming a trefoil. They are narrow and usually pointed. Red clover grows fairly erect and may reach a height of 60cm or more. It is found in grassland and hedgerows. Flowers May–September.

207

Are the petals fused together?

(from 205)

Answer 'Yes' if the petals are fused together so that they cannot easily be distinguished and the flower is shaped more or less like a bell, funnel or tube. Answer 'No' if each petal is clearly distinct down to its base.

Yes 208 No 216

Bell-shaped

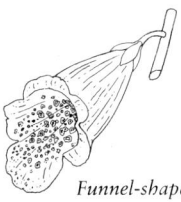

Funnel-shaped

208

Is the plant hairy?

(from 207)

Answer 'Yes' if the leaves and stem are noticeably hairy. Answer 'No' if they are almost or completely hairless, though they may have some soft down.

Yes 209 No 211

209 Are the flowers in a straight, erect spike?

(from 208)

Answer 'Yes' if the stem bearing the flowers is straight and perfectly upright. Answer 'No' if the flowers are in a spirally twisted spike, at least when young.

Yes 210 No 114

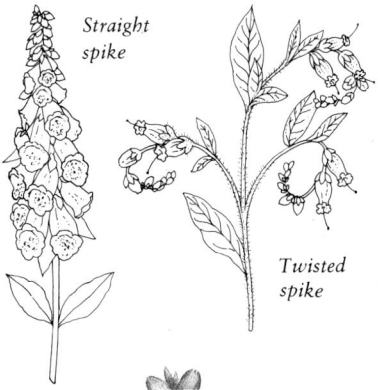

210 FOXGLOVE *(Digitalis purpurea)*

(from 209)

The well-known foxglove is easily recognized with its tall, erect stem, usually unbranched, and its many purple, bell-shaped flowers. It sometimes reaches a height of 150cm. The hairy leaves are toothed and have short stalks. Foxgloves usually grow in woodland. They flower June–August.

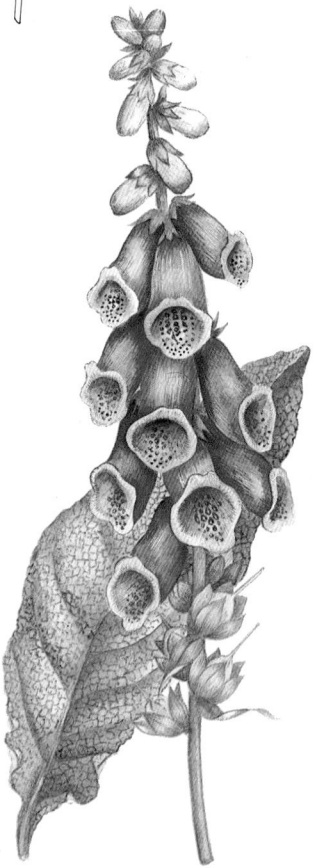

211 Is the plant a climber?

(from 208)

Answer 'Yes' if it grows by twining itself around other vegetation. Answer 'No' if the stem is upright and self-supporting.

Yes 212 No 213

212 FIELD BINDWEED *(Convolvulus arvensis)*

(from 211 and 112)

Field bindweed is unmistakable as it climbs and twists with its pink or white flowers ($1\frac{1}{2}$–3cm) over and around nearby vegetation. The arrow-shaped leaves grow singly, each with its own short stalk. The flowers also have short stalks, and are either single or in pairs. Usually grows in gardens, where it is a common weed, or on farmland or in hedgerows. Flowers June–September.

213 Is the flower 2-lipped?

(from 211)

Answer 'Yes' if the flower has 2 lips. Answer 'No' if it is bell-shaped and hangs down.

Yes 214 No 215

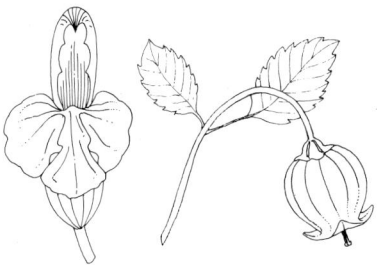

2-lipped flower *Bell-shaped*

214 RED RATTLE *(Pedicularis palustris)*

(from 213)

Red rattle grows with a single upright stem, which is usually purplish. The deeply divided leaves are its most noticeable feature. The pinkish-purple flowers are in a loose spike. Each of them has 2 lips; the upper one is very narrow, the lower one is broad. This plant, also known as marsh lousewort, has a liking for damp ground but will grow in grassland almost anywhere. Flowers May–September.

Field bindweed

Red rattle

215

BILBERRY
(Vaccinium myrtillus)

(from 213)

Bilberries are best known for their delicious, rounded fruit, which turn purple-black when ripe. They develop from small flowers (4–6mm), which grow singly or in pairs on short stalks from the stems. The leaves, which are also short-stalked, are oval and toothed. Bilberries usually grow on moors and mountains, or in dry woodland. Flowers April–June.

fruit

216 How many petals has each flower?

(from 207)

Count the number of petals (or petal-like sepals) in each flower and choose your answer accordingly.

4 217
5 226
6 248
Not clear 226

217 Do the flowers grow singly?

(from 216)

Answer 'Yes' if each flower is solitary, with its own stem to itself. Answer 'No' if several or many flowers grow close together, and the flower-stalks are very short.

Yes 218 No 221

Flower single

Flowers not single

218 Are the petals scarlet?

(from 217)

Answer 'Yes' if the petals are scarlet, usually with a black blotch at their bases. Answer 'No' if they are a paler orange-pink.

Yes 219 No 220

219 COMMON POPPY *(Papaver rhoeas)*

(from 218)

This poppy is extremely distinctive, with its large, scarlet flowers (7–10cm) which have delicate petals and grow singly on long stems. The leaves have deep lobes and are almost stalkless. The smooth seed capsule is noticeably rounded, unlike the long-headed poppy (see 220). Seldom seen in cornfields nowadays, it is found growing on roadsides, on wasteland and along the edges of arable ground. Flowers June–August.

220 LONG-HEADED POPPY *(Papaver dubium)*

(from 218)

Similar to the common poppy (see 219) apart from its paler, smaller flowers (3–7cm) and its more elongated seed capsule.

221 Is the plant growing by the seaside?

(from 217)

Answer 'Yes' if it is growing in sand or shingle not far from the sea. Otherwise answer 'No'.

Yes 222 No 223

222 SEA ROCKET

(Cakile maritima)

(from 221)

This hairless, fleshy plant grows untidily on the seashore. Its stems sprawl along the beach, or along sand dunes or shingle, then rise to bear small clusters of flowers (1–2cm) and deeply divided leaves. The upper leaves are stalkless; the lower ones have short stalks. Flowers June–August.

223 Are the leaves composite?

(from 221)

Answer 'Yes' if each leaf is composed of several separate leaflets. Answer 'No' if the leaves, though they may be deeply divided, are each single and independent.

Yes 224 No 225

Composite *Single*

224 COMMON FUMITORY

(Fumaria officinalis)

(from 223)

The flowers of fumitory (7–10mm long) are in a long spike at the end of the stem, with about 20 tube-like blossoms in each spike. Sometimes the plant grows erect, but more usually it twines itself around nearby vegetation. The fruit is green and spherical. Usually grows on arable land, but is also found on roadsides and wasteland. Flowers May–October. (See opposite.)

225

(from 223)

ROSEBAY WILLOWHERB
(Epilobium angustifolium)

This tall, erect plant bears a family likeness to the two other willowherbs covered in this book (see 265) but the two upper petals of each flower are slightly larger than the two lower ones and the leaves are alternate. The flowers (2–3cm) are rose-purple, with narrow purple sepals between the petals. They form a long conspicuous spike. The leaves are long and narrow. Often found on waste ground, railway sidings or bombsites, but also in woodland and on roadsides. Flowers July–September.

Rosebay willowherb

226

(from 216)

Are the leaves composite?

Answer 'Yes' if each leaf is composed of several separate leaflets, which may be rounded or pointed. Answer 'No' if the leaves, though they may be deeply lobed, are each single and independent.

Yes 227 No 240

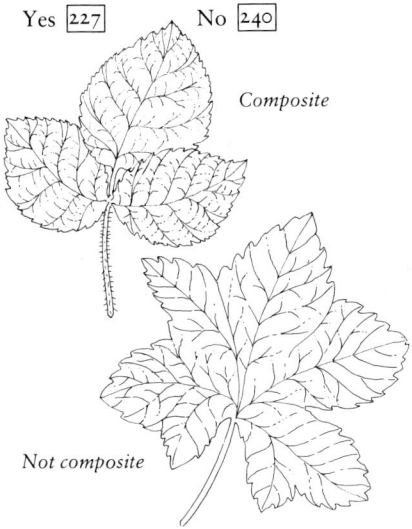

Composite

Not composite

Common fumitory

227 Are the stems thorny?

(from 226)
Answer 'Yes' if all the stems are very noticeably covered with sharp thorns. Answer 'No' if they are thornless.

Yes 228 No 231

228 Are the petals pointed?

(from 227)
Answer 'Yes' if each petal comes to a point. Choose 'No' if each has a noticeable indentation, so that it is more or less heart-shaped.

Yes 229 No 230

Pointed *Heart-shaped*

Bramble

229

BRAMBLE
(Rubus fruticosus)

(from 228 and 121)

There are many different brambles, all generally similar. The differences are too minor and complex for listing in this book. The well-known blackberry is typical of all of them, with its pink or white flowers (2–3cm), its thorny, arching stems, and above all its delicious fruit, which ripens from green to red to black. Brambles grow in hedgerows, on waste ground and in woodland. They flower May–September.

230

DOG ROSE
(Rosa canina)

(from 228)

Dog rose is very conspicuous, as it climbs over nearby vegetation with its handsome pink flowers (4–5cm), each of which has 5 heart-shaped petals. The composite leaves have 5–7 toothed leaflets, which are usually hairless, as is the thorny stem. The fruit is the well-known scarlet hip. Dog roses grow in hedgerows and woodland. They flower June–July.

Dog rose

231 Is the plant a climber?

(from 227)

Answer 'Yes' if it grows by twining and self-supporting.
Answer 'No' if the stem is upright

Yes 232 No 233

232

(from 231)

COMMON VETCH
(Vicia sativa)
BUSH VETCH
(Vicia sepium)

These two purple vetches are similar and it is best to take them together. The main difference is that the flowers of common vetch usually grow singly or in pairs whilst bush vetch's are in small clusters of 2–6. Both have tendrils at their leaf tips, enabling them to clamber round nearby vegetation, and 3–9 pairs of leaflets in each leaf, forming a regular pattern. Both plants are found in grassland and hedgerows. They flower May–September.

Note that another common member of the family, tufted vetch, has much bluer flowers and is not therefore included in this section (see 330).

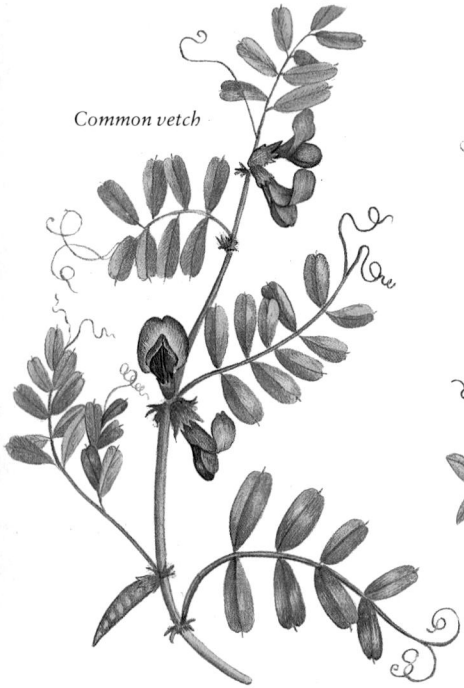

233 Are the flowers shaped like those of a pea?

(from 231)

Answer 'Yes' if the irregular flowers are shaped like a pea's (see illustration). Otherwise answer 'No'.

Yes 234 No 235

Pea-like flower

234 RESTHARROW *(Ononis repens)*

(from 233)

The stems of restharrow lie creeping along the ground, except towards the ends which usually turn upwards to bear the flowers. These grow on short stalks from the points in the stem where the leaves join it. The toothed leaves may grow singly, in pairs or in threes. The whole plant is hairy. It often grows on sand dunes by the sea, but also in grassland or scrub. Flowers June–September.

235 Are the leaflets opposite?

(from 233)

Answer 'Yes' if the leaflets are borne in opposite pairs along the leaf-stalk. Answer 'No' if they radiate from the tip of the leaf-stalk like the fingers of your hand.

Yes 236 No 239

Opposite leaflets

Radiating leaflets

236 Do the flowers hang down?

(from 235)

Answer 'Yes' if the flowers hang on long, slender stalks. Answer 'No' if they are borne on straight stalks and face upwards.

Yes 237 No 238

237 WATER AVENS
(Geum rivale)

(from 236)

The flowers hang singly, each from its own slender stalk towards the end of the stem. They are pinkish with 5 rounded petals, surrounded by 5 prominent purple sepals. The composite leaves are composed of toothed leaflets in opposite pairs; the end leaflet is the largest. The whole plant is hairy. Water avens grows in damp woodlands as well as in shady places near water and in hedgerows. Flowers May–September.

Water avens

Common stork's-bill

238 COMMON STORK'S-BILL
(Erodium cicutarium)

(from 236)

This plant resembles the well-known herb-robert (see 239) apart from its pointed petals and the arrangement of its leaves. These are divided into many leaflets growing in opposite pairs, and the leaflets themselves are similarly divided. The small pink flowers (12–14mm) are in loose clusters of 2–5, each with an individual stalk. They develop into long, beaked fruits. Stork's-bill likes sandy ground and often grows by the sea-shore or in dry fields. Flowers June–September.

6/12 Grasmere. Cumbria

239

HERB-ROBERT
(Geranium robertianum)

(from 235)

The bright pink flowers have rounded petals and grow singly or in loose clusters. The leaves are composed of 3 or 5 leaflets and the leaflets are deeply divided. Some stems may be upright but they are inclined to straggle, so that a plant covers a wide area. The stem, stalks and leaves turn noticeably red as summer progresses. Often grows on walls or in stony places, also in woodland. Flowers May–September.

240 Are the leaves lobed?

(from 226)

Answer 'Yes' if there are several deep indentations in the margins of each leaf. These are known as lobes. Answer 'No' if the margins are not indented, though they may be toothed.

Yes 241 No 242

Unlobed

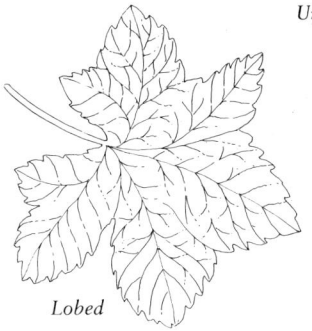

Lobed

241 **COMMON MALLOW**
(Malva sylvestris)
(from 240)

The pink heart-shaped petals are quite narrow at their bases, so that each is distinct from its neighbour. The flowers ($2\frac{1}{2}$–4cm) grow in small clusters of 2–5 blooms, each with its individual stalk. The clusters rise from the points where the leaf-stalks join the stem. Sometimes the plant is hairy but this is variable. Mallows prefer dry ground and grow in open country on arable ground or wasteland. They flower June–September.

242 Are the leaves fleshy?
(from 240)
Answer 'Yes' if the toothed leaves are noticeably thick and fleshy. Otherwise answer 'No'.

Yes 243 No 244

243 **ORPINE**
(Sedum telephium)
(from 242)

Orpine usually has several upright, unbranched stems growing quite close together. They are often tinged with red; the toothed, unstalked leaves are arranged alternately along them. The rose-red flowers (9–12mm) are in close, rounded clusters at the end of the stems. It is almost always found in woods and hedgerows. Flowers July–September.

244 Are the leaves stalkless?

(from 242)
Answer 'Yes' if the leaves have no stalks, or extremely short ones. Answer 'No' if leaf stalks are definitely present.

Yes 245 No 246

245 REDSHANK
(Polygonum persicaria)

(from 244)

The tiny pink flowers grow in very compact spikes. The largest spike is at the head of the stem, with the others, if any, from stalks branching to each side of it. The leaves are narrow and taper to a point; they often have black blotches on them. Redshank is a weed of cultivated ground or grassland. Usually prefers a damp site. Flowers June–October.

246 Is the plant a climber?

(from 244)
Answer 'Yes' if it grows by twining itself around other vegetation. Otherwise answer 'No'.

Yes 125 No 247

247 AMPHIBIOUS BISTORT
(Polygonum amphibium)

(from 246)

This plant occurs in two different forms. Either it grows in water, with its roots completely submerged and its leaves floating on the water, or on damp ground, usually near a river, when its stem is mostly procumbent, lying along the ground and putting out roots at intervals. Otherwise it is extremely like redshank (see 245) apart from its stalked leaves. Flowers July–September.

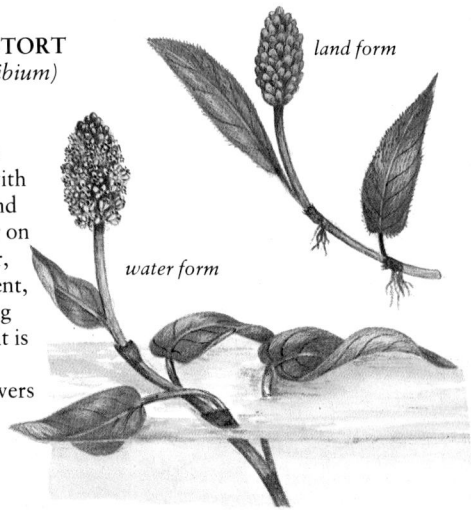

248 Is it broad-leaved?

(from 216)

Answer 'Yes' if at least some of the leaves are less than twice as long as they are broad. Answer 'No' if all of them are narrow.

Yes 249 No 250

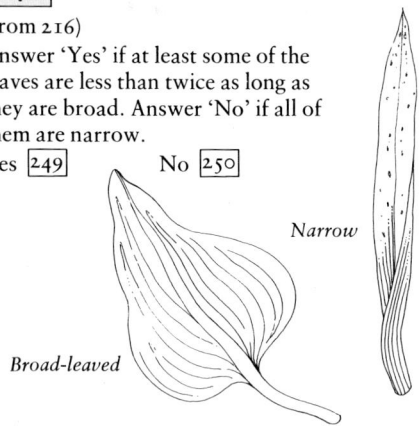

249 BROAD-LEAVED HELLEBORINE *(Epipactis helleborine)*

(from 248)

This orchid is distinguished by the relatively broad leaves growing towards the base of its erect stem. The flowers, which are greenish red, are in a long loose spike, all to one side of the stem. Broad-leaved helleborine may reach a height of 80cm. It grows in woods or hedgerows. Flowers July–October.

250 Does each flower have a long, narrow spur?

(from 248)

The remaining three species covered are all orchids, whose flowers are in quite a dense spike at the top of a single, erect stem. Examine a flower carefully and answer 'Yes' if there is a narrow spur, 11–13mm in length, pointing downwards and backwards from its base. Answer 'No' if the spur is shorter and more rounded.

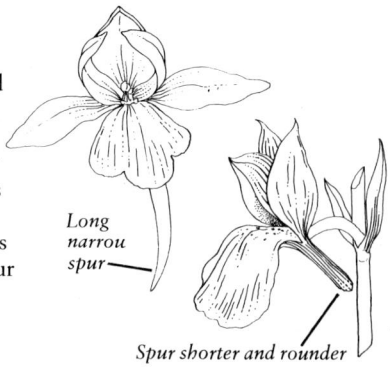

Yes 251 No 252

251

(from 250)

FRAGRANT ORCHID
(Gymnadenia conopsea)

As its name indicates, this orchid is sweet-smelling, especially in the evening. Like other orchids, it is hairless and has narrow, pointed leaves embracing the stem, especially towards its base. The flowers vary from quite pale pink to magenta. This plant usually grows on dry grassland, occasionally in marshes. Flowers June–July.

252

(from 250)

Do the flowers have long green bracts?

A bract looks exactly like a small, pointed leaf. Answer 'Yes' if, along the whole length of the flowering spike, there are many prominent green bracts intermingled with the blooms. Answer 'No' if the spikes of flowers have inconspicuous bracts the same colour as the stem.

Yes 253 No 254

253

(from 252)

COMMON SPOTTED ORCHID
(Dactylorhiza fuchsii)

The flowers of common spotted orchid are usually pink, but they may be pinkish-white or even pure white. The leaves growing at the base of the plant are less narrow than those higher up the stem, which they embrace. In both cases they may have black spots (as in the illustration) but these are sometimes absent. Usually found in open woods and grassland. Flowers June–August.

254

EARLY PURPLE ORCHID
(Orchis mascula)

(from 252)

This is the first orchid to be seen in bloom in springtime. The flowers are usually bright purple, but may be much lighter coloured. The leaves are quite similar to those of the common spotted orchid (see 253) and, again, may or may not have black spots. The single stems are hairless and erect. Usually found in open woods or scrub, occasionally in grassland. Flowers April–June.

255

Are the flowers regular?

(from 192)

Answer 'Yes' if all the petals of each flower are equal in size and the same shape. Otherwise answer 'No'.

Yes 256 No 275

256

Are the leaves composite?

(from 255)

Answer 'Yes' if each leaf is composed of several separate leaflets; 'No' if the leaves are each single and independent.

Yes 257 No 260

257

Are the leaflets opposite?

(from 256)

Answer 'Yes' if the leaflets are in opposite pairs along the leaf stalk. Answer 'No' if all or most of the leaves are composed of 3 leaflets, which grow in opposite pairs along the stem.

Yes 258 No 259

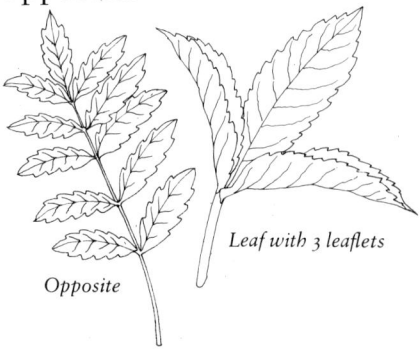

258

COMMON VALERIAN
(Valeriana officinalis)

(from 257)

Valerian grows erect with a single stem, usually unbranched. Its compound leaves are composed of small leaflets, which grow in opposite pairs and may or may not be toothed. The leaves at the base of the plant have noticeable stalks but these get progressively shorter. The small pink flowers (5mm) grow in tight clusters. Valerian prefers a damp site and grows in grassland or wasteland. Flowers June–August.

259

HEMP-AGRIMONY
(Eupatorium cannabinum)

(from 257)

This tall plant (30–170cm) usually grows with several upright stems, which are sometimes tinged with pink. Each flowerhead is composed of 5–6 very small tubular florets, and several flowerheads are grouped together to form loose clusters. The stem leaves are divided into 3 toothed leaflets, which are almost stalkless and arranged in opposite pairs. Hemp-agrimony grows on damp ground and flowers July–September.

260

How many petals has each flower?

(from 256)

Count the number of petals in each flower and choose your answer accordingly.

4 261
5 266
6 274

261 Are the flowers bell-shaped?

(from 260)

Answer 'Yes' if the petals of each flower are fused together in the shape of a bell or tube, so that no individual petals can be clearly distinguished. Otherwise answer 'No'.

Yes 262 No 263

Bell-shaped

262

(from 261)

BELL HEATHER
(Erica cinerea)
CROSS-LEAVED HEATH
(Erica tetralix)

These two heathers are distinguished from the third species most commonly seen (see 264) by their bell-shaped flowers. The two species are rather similar and it is best to take them together. The main difference is that the leaves of the bell heather are in whorls of 3 around their stems, whilst those of the cross-leaved heath are in whorls of 4. Also the latter's flowers tend to be purple, whilst those of the bell heather are more of a rose-pink. Both species grow on acid ground, usually moorland or mountain. Flowers June–September.

Bell heather

Cross-leaved heath

263 Is the stem woody?

(from 261)

Answer 'Yes' if the plant is a heather, with a thick bushy growth and a tough woody stem. Otherwise answer 'No'.

Yes 264 No 265

264

(from 263)

HEATHER
(Calluna vulgaris)

This heather, also known as ling, should be distinguished from the two species with bell-shaped flowers (see 262). The flowers, which grow in close spikes at the end of woody stems, have 4 clearly defined petals when fully opened. The tiny leaves (1–2mm) are stalkless and arranged in opposite pairs, not whorled. The whole plant is often bushy. Heather grows on acid ground, almost always mountain or moorland. Flowers July–September.

265

(from 263)

GREAT WILLOWHERB
(Epilobium hirsutum)
BROAD-LEAVED WILLOWHERB
(Epilobium montanum)

Many species of willowherb, all rather similar, are found in the British Isles, but only the three commonest are covered in this book. One of these has alternate leaves and slightly irregular flowers and is therefore not included in this section (see 225). The two remaining species are taken together here to assist identification.

Both are erect plants with flowers in loose clusters on individual stems. The main difference is that the flowers of great willowherb (15–23mm) are larger and more purple than those of broad-leaved willowherb (6–9mm). The leaves in both cases are toothed, but broad-leaved willowherb's have very

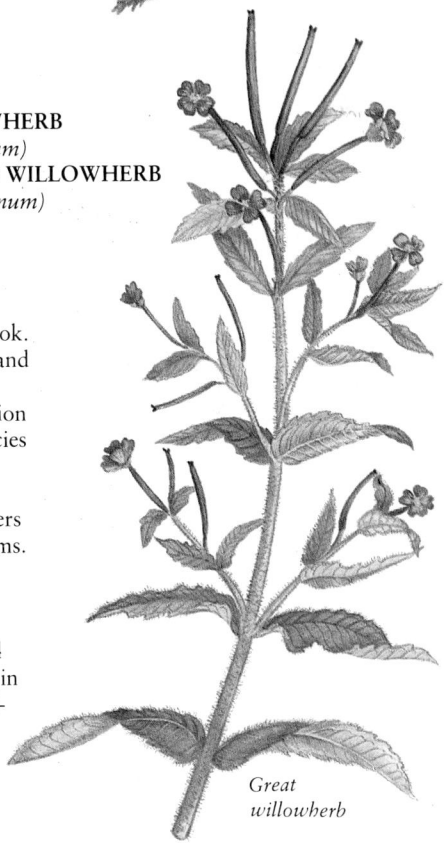

Great willowherb

definite stalks, whilst great willowherb's are almost or completely stalkless. A final important distinction is that great willowherb is almost always found in damp places, often by a river, whilst broad-leaved willowherb prefers shady hedgerows, gardens and wasteland. Both flower June–August.

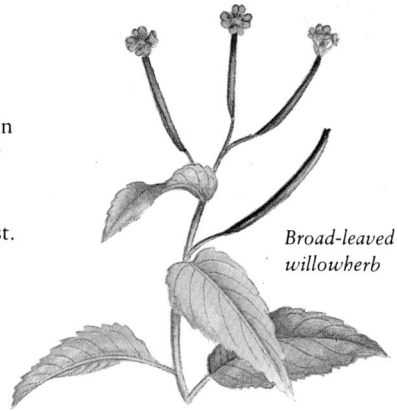

Broad-leaved willowherb

266 What size are the flowers?

(from 260)

Measure the diameter of an average flower and choose your answer accordingly.

Up to 5mm 267
10–15mm 268
Over 18mm 271

267 SAND SPURREY *(Spergularia rubra)*

(from 266)

This little plant has many sprawling stems and seldom stands erect. Its flowers are very small and so are its leaves. The flowers (3–5mm) are pink and star-like with undivided petals and prominent green sepals; they grow singly on individual stalks. The leaves are very narrow and sharp pointed, growing in whorls around the stems. Sand spurrey likes lime-free soil and is found growing in sandy ground especially in grassland and wasteland. Flowers May–September.

268 Is the plant prostrate?

(from 266)

Answer 'Yes' if, for most of its length, the stem is lying prostrate along the ground. Answer 'No' if it is erect.

Yes 269 No 270

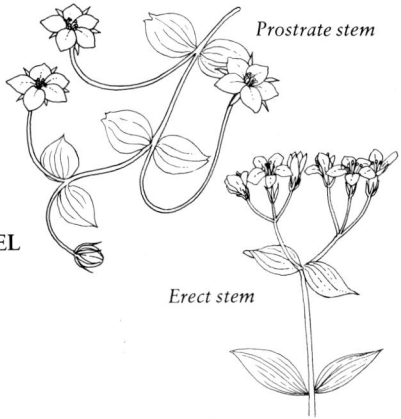

269 SCARLET PIMPERNEL

(Anagallis arvensis)

(from 268)

The bright red, star-like flowers (10–15mm) are scarlet pimpernel's most conspicuous feature. They grow singly on individual stalks, rising from the prostrate stem, which is square in cross-section. The stalkless leaves are oval and pointed. The whole plant is hairless. Scarlet pimpernels are usually found in grassland, or may grow on sand dunes. They flower June–August.

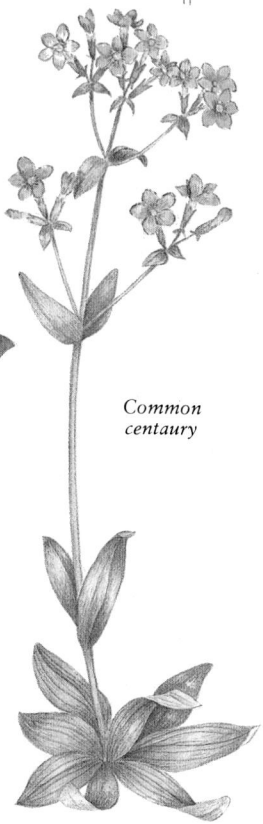

270 COMMON CENTAURY

(Centaurium erythraea)

(from 268)

Centaury grows erect, with a hairless, branching stem. The flowers (10–15mm) are in quite loose clusters without noticeable stalks. The paired leaves, which are stalkless, may be either rounded or pointed. This plant is found in dry grassland or on sand dunes. Flowers June–October.

271 Are the leaves hairless?

(from 266)

Answer 'Yes' if the leaves, though they may be rough to the touch, are completely without hairs. Answer 'No' if they are hairy.

Yes 272 No 273

272 RAGGED-ROBIN *(Lychnis flos-cuculi)*

(from 271)

Each of the rose-red petals is extremely deeply divided into four very narrow segments. The flowers grow in a very loose cluster, sometimes singly, each with its own stalk. The paired leaves are narrow and pointed; the lower ones are stalked. Ragged-robin prefers damp ground and is usually found in water meadows and moist woodland. Flowers May–August.

Ragged-robin

273 RED CAMPION *(Silene dioica)*

(from 271)

The petals are heart-shaped. At the base of each flower (18–25mm) there is a hairy brown tube. The flowers grow in small, loose clusters at the end of erect stems. The upper leaves, but not the lower ones, are stalkless. Usually found in woodland edges and hedgerows. Flowers May–June.

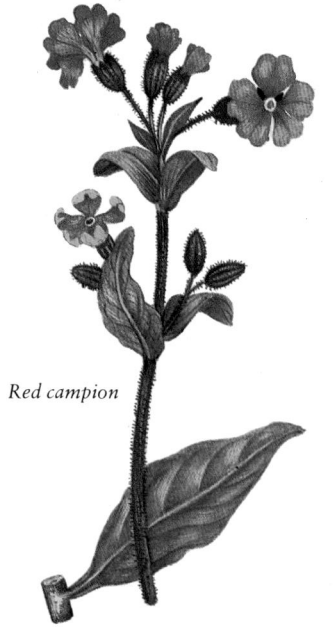

Red campion

274 PURPLE LOOSESTRIFE *(Lythrum salicaria)*

(from 260)

This plant is very conspicuous, with its tall erect stem and the very long spike of stalkless, purple flowers

(10–15mm) growing in whorls around it. The stem is square and hairless. There are short, pointed bracts, looking like small leaves, below each whorl of flowers. The leaves grow in opposite pairs or in whorls of 3; they are untoothed, narrow and stalkless. Purple loosestrife almost always grows in damp places, often close to water. Flowers June–August.

Purple loosestrife

275 Is the plant a climber?

(from 255)

Answer 'Yes' if it grows by twining itself around other vegetation. Answer 'No' if the stem is upright and self-supporting.

Yes 70 No 276

276 Are the leaves hairless?

(from 275)

Answer 'Yes' if the leaves are completely without hairs. Answer 'No' if they are noticeably downy.

Yes 277 No 278

277 COMMON FIGWORT *(Scrophularia nodosa)*

(from 276)

The small flowers of the figwort are not at all conspicuous. Partly reddish-brown and partly green, they grow in open clusters from the branching head of the stem. The leaves are pointed and toothed. Figwort likes damp ground and grows in moist woodland or hedgerows. Flowers June–September.

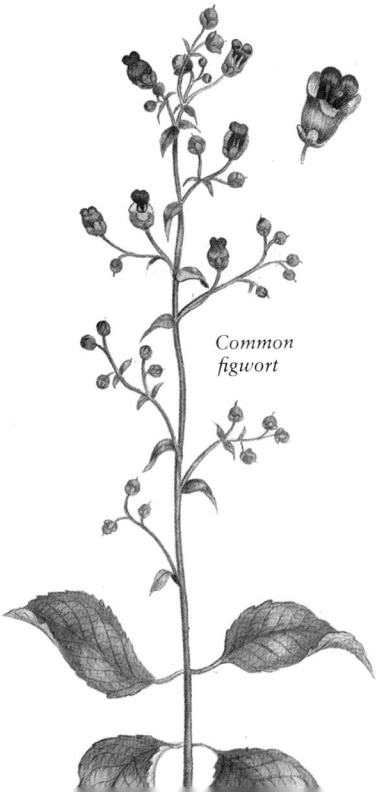

Common figwort

278 Do the flowers grow in separate whorls?

(from 276)

Answer 'Yes' if the flowers grow in separate whorls around the stem. Answer 'No' if all the whorls grow together in a loose spike at the top of the stem.

Yes 279 No 280

279 RED DEAD-NETTLE *(Lamium purpureum)*

(from 278)

This plant seldom has many flowers. They grow in little whorls around the stem, with a pair of leaves underneath each whorl. The leaves, which are stalked and toothed, are heart-shaped or may be rounded. They do not sting. The red dead-nettle grows more or less erect but does not exceed 30cm in height. It grows on arable land as well as on wasteground and in hedgerows. Flowers March–October.

Red dead-nettle

280 COMMON HEMP-NETTLE *(Galeopsis tetrahit)* HEDGE WOUNDWORT *(Stachys sylvatica)*

(from 278)

These 2 species are quite similar and it is convenient to take them together. In both cases, the purple flowers grow in whorls forming a loose spike at the end of the stem, with a small pair of leaves below each whorl. The leaves of hedge woundwort are heart-shaped and generally have longer stalks. The best distinguishing feature is that hemp-nettle's stem is noticeably swollen beneath each point where the leaf-stalks joins it, whereas woundwort's is straight-sided. In both cases, the stems are noticeably hairy. Woundwort has a preference for shady places in woods and hedgerows; hemp-nettle is also found on arable land. Both flower July–September.

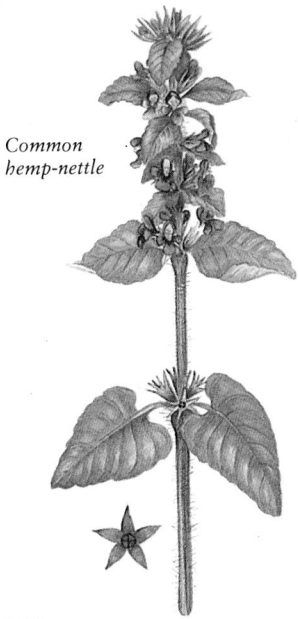

Common hemp-nettle

Hedge woundwort

281 Does each flower have three petals?

(from 192)

This question needs no elaboration.

Yes 282 No 287

282 Are the leaves very long and narrow?

(from 281)

Answer 'Yes' if the leaves are extremely narrow, many times longer than they are broad, and much the same breadth for all their length. Otherwise answer 'No'.

Yes 283 No 284

283 (from 282)

FLOWERING-RUSH
(Butomus umbellatus)

This waterside plant is at once recognized by its handsome pink flowers, which grow in a cluster, each with its own stalk, at the end of the unbranched stems. The narrow leaves have triangular cross-sections and usually grow taller than the stems, perhaps to 100cm. Always found in or beside water. Flowers June–August.

284 (from 282)

Are the leaves shaped like arrowheads?

Answer 'Yes' if the plant has leaves of an unusual shape, resembling arrowheads. Answer 'No' if they are oval with pointed tips.

Yes 285 No 286

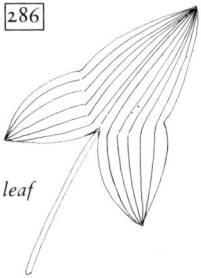

Arrowhead-like leaf

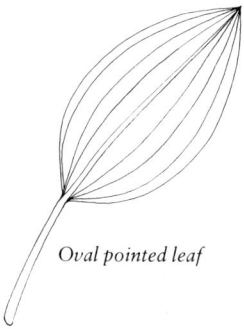

Oval pointed leaf

285 (from 284 and 89)

ARROWHEAD
(Sagittaria sagittifolia)

The flowers (3cm) are white with purple centres. They grow in whorls of 3–5, forming a loose spike at the end of each flowering stem. The hairless leaves have very long stalks.

Arrowhead always grows in water. Some leaves are submerged below the surface; these are very long and narrow but you probably will not see them. Flowers July–August.

286

WATER-PLANTAIN
(Alisma plantago-aquatica)

(from 284)

The flowers (10mm) may be pale pink or white. They grow on quite long stalks in whorled clusters from branches at the end of the stems. The leaves have long stalks and are oval with pointed tips. Always found growing in or near water. Flowers June–August.

287

Is the plant growing in or beside water?

(from 281)

Answer 'Yes' if at least the root of the plant is growing in water, or if it is close beside a river or lake, or in a marsh or swamp. Answer 'No' if it is growing on dry land.

Yes 288 No 289

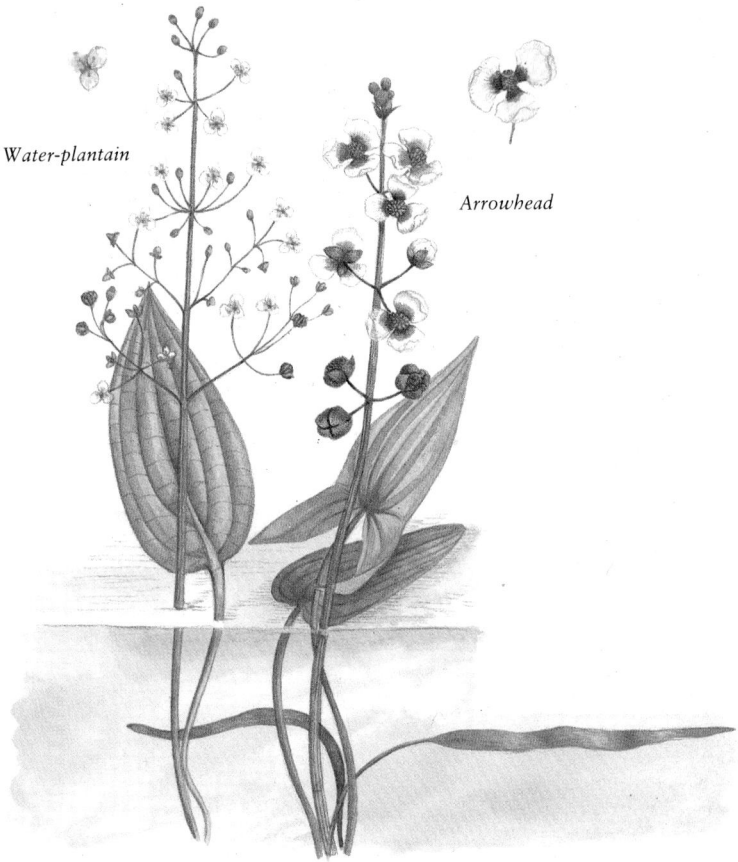

288

BOGBEAN
(Menyanthes trifoliata)

(from 287)

This handsome water plant has distinctive flowers and leaves. The flowers (15mm) are pink and white; their 5 petals form a star and they are covered with cottony hairs. They grow in a loose cluster at the end of a long stem. The leaves are each divided into 3 large oval leaflets at the ends of separate stalks, rising up from the roots. Bogbean always grows in or beside water, or on very wet bogland. Flowers May–July.

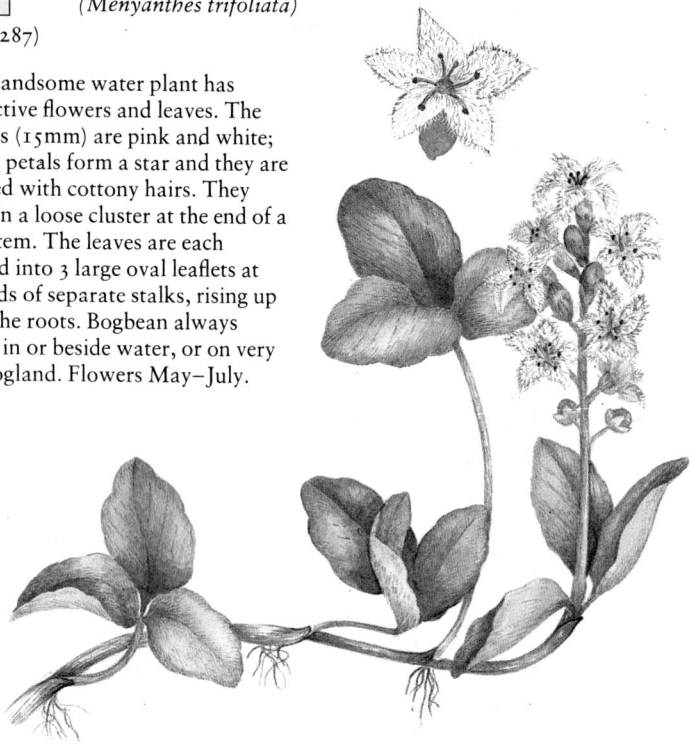

289

Does each plant have many crowded flowerheads?

(from 287)

Answer 'Yes' if each stout, straight stem is topped with a close-growing mass of crowded rounded flowerheads, each comprising many flowers. Answer 'No' if each stem has a single flowerhead.

Yes 290 No 291

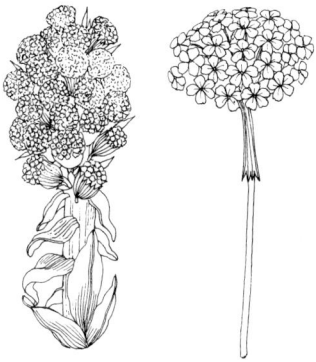

Many crowded flowerheads *Single flowerhead*

290

(from 289 and 188)

BUTTERBUR
(Petasites hybridus)

The very small pinkish flowers grow close together in flowerheads, which are grouped to form clusters at the end of short, erect stems. The flowers come out just before the leaves, which are heart-shaped or kidney-shaped, with prominent teeth and stalks. Butterbur grows in damp places, in meadows, open woodland or on roadsides. Flowers March–May.

291

(from 289)

THRIFT
(Armeria maritima)

The small flowers (8mm) grow in dense rounded clusters, with a single cluster at the end of each leafless stem. The long narrow leaves, which may or may not be hairy, are in bluish-green tufts at the bases of the stems. Thrift is usually found by the seaside, but also grows on mountains, salt marshes and even in meadows. Flowers April–October.

292

(from 1)

Are the flowers in dense rounded flowerheads?

Answer 'Yes' if numerous very small flowers are packed close together to form a dense rounded flowerhead. Otherwise answer 'No'.

Yes 293 No 298

293 Are the leaves prickly?

(from 292)
This question needs no elaboration.

Yes 294 No 295

294 SEA HOLLY
(Eryngium maritimum)

(from 293)

Many very small flowers (8mm) are crowded together to form the unmistakable rounded flowerheads of sea holly. At the base of each flowerhead grows a circle of spiny bracts, looking like small leaves. The true leaves are stalkless, except those at the base. The whole plant is hairless. Sea holly always grows by the coast, usually in sand or shingle. Flowers July–August.

295 Are all the flowers much the same size?

(from 293)
Answer 'Yes' if all the little flowers composing each flowerhead are more or less the same size. Answer 'No' if those at the rim of each flowerhead are noticeably larger than those at the centre.

Yes 296 No 297

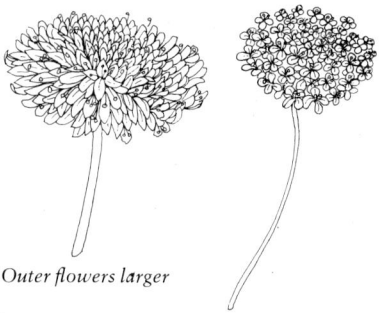

Outer flowers larger

All flowers much the same size

296 DEVIL'S-BIT SCABIOUS
(Succisa pratensis)

(from 295)

The flowerheads (15–25mm) are smaller than those of field scabious (see 297) but the same shape and colour. They grow at the end of long delicate stems, which are usually branched. The narrow, pointed leaves grow in opposite pairs and may be slightly hairy. Usually found in grassland or damp woodland. Flowers June–October.

297

FIELD SCABIOUS
(Knautia arvensis)

(from 295)

Very similar to devil's-bit scabious (see 296) but with larger flowerheads (3–4cm) and deeply divided leaves. This erect plant may reach a height of 100cm. It has hairy leaves and stems, which sometimes become bristly. Field scabious usually grows in grassland and hedgerows. Flowers July–September.

Devil's-bit scabious

Field scabious

298 Are the flowers regular?

(from 292)

Answer 'Yes' if all the petals of each flower are more or less equal in size and the same shape. Answer 'No' if the flowers are so irregular that they can only be divided in 2 equal halves in one direction. (Note that the tiny flowers of the mints appear regular until examined closely with a magnifying glass, but their irregularity is so slight that they should be classed as regular.)

Yes 299 No 322

299 Does the plant smell of mint?

(from 298)

Crush a leaf between finger and thumb and smell it. Answer 'Yes' if it has a strong smell of mint; otherwise answer 'No'.

Yes 319 No 300

300 Are the flowers bell-shaped?

(from 299)

Answer 'Yes' if the flowers are shaped more or less like a bell: the petals are fused together or so closely overlapping that they cannot easily be distinguished. Answer 'No' if each petal is clearly distinct down to its base.

Yes 301 No 305

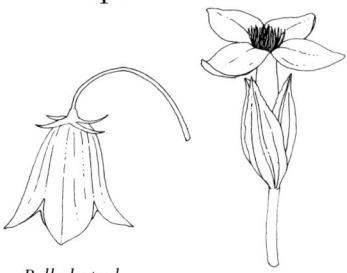

Bell-shaped *Not bell-shaped*

301 Are the leaves basal only?

(from 300)

Answer 'Yes' if the leaves grow only at the base of the plant, so that the flowering stems are leafless. Answer 'No' if leaves also grow from the stems.

Yes 302 No 303

6/12 Grassmere, Cumbria

302

BLUEBELL
(Hyacinthoides non-scripta)

(from 301)

The bluebell (known in Scotland as the hyacinth) is one of the best known and most welcome flowers, carpeting the woodland floor with its bright blue, sweet-scented blossoms in early spring. The flowers dangle in a loose cluster, all facing the same way, at the top of the unbranched stem. The leaves are long and very narrow. The whole plant is hairless. Usually found in deciduous woodland, also in hedgerows and grassland. Flowers April–June.

303

Is the plant bristly?

(from 301)
Answer 'Yes' if the plant is covered in short, stiff, bristly hairs. Otherwise answer 'No'.

Yes 114 No 304

304

HAREBELL
(Campanula rotundifolia)

(from 303)

The harebell (known in Scotland as the bluebell) is perhaps the most bell-like of all flowers. The rim of each blossom is edged with 5 pointed lobes. The flowers grow singly, at intervals along the stem, from short, delicate stalks. The stem leaves are alternate, quite short and very narrow. There are also small round leaves at the base of the plant. Harebells grow on grassland and heathland. Flowers July–September.

Basal leaves

305 How many petals has each flower?

(from 300)

Count the number of petals in each flower and choose your answer accordingly.

4 306
5 312
Over 6 317

306 How big are the flowers?

(from 305)

Measure the diameter of an average-sized flower and choose your answer accordingly.

3mm 307
more than 10mm 308

307 FIELD MADDER

(Sherardia arvensis)

(from 306)

The tiny lilac flowers (2–3mm), which have long petal tubes at their bases, grow in close clusters at the very ends of the stems. The stems are 4-sided and most of them are prostrate (lying along the ground). The pointed leaves grow in whorls of 4–6 and have slightly prickly edges. Field madder grows on farmland or wasteland. Flowers May–October.

308 Are the leaves bristly?

(from 306)

Answer 'Yes' if the leaves are covered in short, stiff, bristly hairs. Otherwise answer 'No'.

Yes 117 No 309

309 Are the leaves compound?

(from 308)

Answer 'Yes' if the lower leaves bear opposite pairs of leaflets. Answer 'No' if the leaves are simple.

Yes 310 No 311

310 (from 309 and 116)

CUCKOO FLOWER
(Cardamine pratensis)

The flowers (12–18mm) range in colour from lilac to rose-pink to white, but those on the same plant are always much the same. They are grouped in quite small clusters at the end of each stem. The leaves are divided into 3–7 rounded leaflets except the upper ones, which are long and narrow. The whole plant is hairless. Cuckoo flower prefers a damp site and often grows by rivers or in damp meadows or woodland. Flowers April–June.

311 (from 309)

FIELD GENTIAN
(Gentianella campestris)

The 4 petals are joined at their bases to form a tube, which is partly hidden by 4 conspicuous sepals. The flowers (15mm) are in quite compact small clusters at the end of the stem or its branches. The hairless, stalkless leaves are oval and pointed. Field gentians grow in grassland or on sand dunes. Rare in southern England. Flowers July–October.

312 (from 305)

Is the plant a climber?

Answer 'Yes' if it grows by twining itself around other vegetation. Answer 'No' if the stem is upright and self-supporting.

Yes 313 No 314

313

BITTERSWEET
(Solanum dulcamara)

(from 312)

The strongly contrasting colours of the flowers – bluish-purple petals with bright yellow anthers in the centre – make bittersweet easy to recognize. The flowers grow in little clusters from quite long stalks as the plant climbs and clambers over surrounding vegetation to a height of 200cm. The leaves are oval and pointed. Bittersweet, also known as woody nightshade, is usually found in woodland and hedgerows, but also has a liking for beaches and sand dunes. Flowers June–September.

314

Are the leaves broad?

(from 312)

Answer 'Yes' if the leaves are almost rounded in outline while at the same time deeply lobed. Answer 'No' if they are short, narrow and unlobed.

Yes 315 No 316

315

MEADOW CRANE'S-BILL
(Geranium pratense)

(from 314)

The large, sky-blue flowers (15–18mm) of meadow crane's-bill are very easy to recognize. They grow singly on quite short stalks towards the ends of the stems. The deeply divided leaves are noticeably hairy; those at the base of the plant are stalked. Usually grows in meadows or other grassland. Flowers June–September.

6/12 Grassmere, Cumbria

316

FIELD FORGET-ME-NOT
(Myosotis arvensis)

(from 314)

The little pale blue flowers (5mm) with yellow centres are very noticeable. They grow in loose spikes at the ends of the branched stems. The whole plant is hairy and grows fairly erect. The leaves are small, undivided and stalkless. Found in dry grassland, roadsides and hedges. Flowers April–September.

(Note that there are several other species of forget-me-not, all rather similar, in particular the water forget-me-not *(Myosotis scorpioides)*, which has larger flowers and grows in damp places; but these are not covered in this book.)

317

Is the plant in fresh water?

(from 305)

Answer 'Yes' if it is growing almost submerged in fresh water. Answer 'No' if it is not far from the sea or by an estuary.

Yes 90 No 318

318

SEA ASTER
(Aster tripolium)

(from 317)

The decorative mauve flowers with yellow centres (8–20mm) make this seem like a garden flower. They grow in loose clusters on individual stalks at the ends of the flowering stems. The hairless, fleshy leaves are narrow and pointed. As its name indicates, this plant is almost always found by the seaside. Flowers July–October.

319 Does each stem end in a flowerhead?

(from 299)

Answer 'Yes' if the largest or only flowerhead grows at the very end of the stem. Answer 'No' if the flowers are in whorls around the stem, with none growing at its tip.

Yes 320 No 321

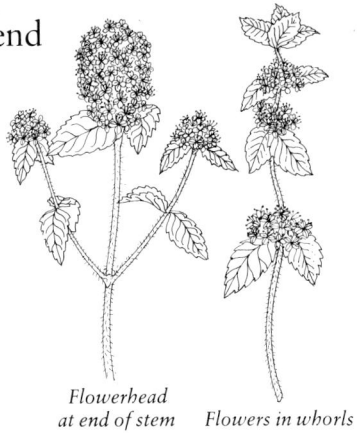

320 WATER MINT *(Mentha aquatica)*

(from 319)

Water mint almost always grows in water, or in wet ground close to water. In addition to the main dense flowerhead at the end of its square stem, there may be flowers in smaller whorls around it, with a pair of leaves below each whorl. The plant is aromatic: its leaves, which are bluntly toothed, have a pleasant minty smell when crushed. Flowers July–October.

321 CORN MINT *(Mentha arvensis)*

(from 319)

Corn mint bears a strong family likeness to water mint (see 320) with its square stem, downy leaves and small lilac flowers, but the flowers are in a series of whorls along the stem, with a pair of leaves under each whorl, and there is no flowerhead at the end of the stem. The leaves of the corn mint give off a faint minty smell when crushed. The plant likes damp ground, but not as wet as water mint. Found as a weed in arable ground or in damp woods and meadows. Flowers May–October.

322 How do the leaves grow?

(from 298)

Leaves are described as being alternate, opposite, whorled or basal, depending on how they are arranged along their stem or stalk. The drawings will help you to decide.

Alternate leaves grow singly, on alternating sides of the stem, while opposite leaves are in pairs. Choose 'Basal only' if all the leaves grow at the very base of the plant.

Alternate 323
Opposite 334
Basal only 341

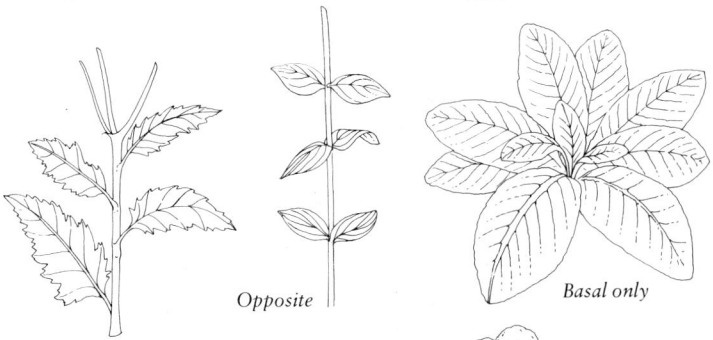

Alternate *Opposite* *Basal only*

323 Do the flowers grow singly?

(from 322)

Answer 'Yes' if each flower is solitary, with its own stalk to itself. Answer 'No' if several or many flowers grow close together; the flower-stalks, if any, are very short.

Yes 324 No 329

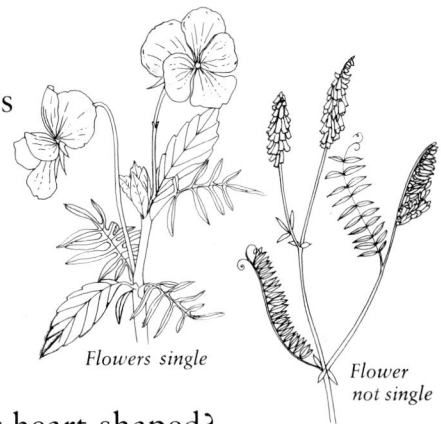

Flowers single *Flower not single*

324 Are the leaves heart-shaped?

(from 323)

Answer 'Yes' if the leaves are rounded, but have indentations and come to a point so that they are more or less heart-shaped. Otherwise answer 'No'.

Yes 325 No 326

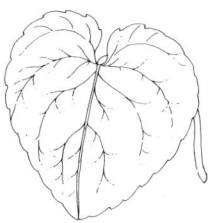

325

COMMON DOG VIOLET
(Viola riviniana)

(from 324)

Of the two best-known violets, sweet violet has all its leaves at the base of the plant and is therefore considered separately (see 341). Dog violet is scentless, unlike sweet violet, and has rather larger flowers (up to 25mm). Its hairless leaves grow from delicate stalks, either from the base of the plant or along the stems. Dog violet grows on woodland banks, in woods or shady grassland. Flowers April–June.

326

Does the plant stand erect?

(from 324)
Answer 'Yes' if its stem is strong enough to stand upright. Answer 'No' if the whole plant is prostrate, crawling low over the ground.

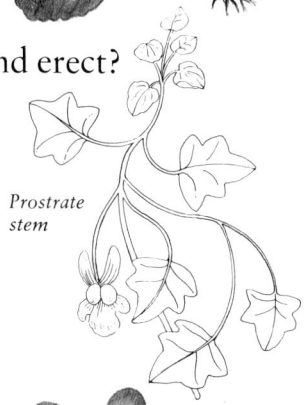

Yes 327 No 328

327

WILD PANSY
(Viola tricolor)

(from 57 and 326)

The flowers of wild pansy are variable in colour: they may be violet, yellow, or a combination of both. They grow singly on a delicate stalk from the fairly erect, leafy stem. There are deeply divided leaf-like stipules at the bases of the flower-stalks. Pansies grow on arable ground, wasteland or dry grassland. Flowers April–September.

328 IVY-LEAVED TOADFLAX
(Cymbalaria muralis)

(from 326)

This plant is distinctive because it almost always grows on walls or stone steps, though it may also thrive on rocks or stony ground. The very small leaves are indeed ivy-shaped, with conspicuous pointed lobes. The flowers, too, are very small (5–10mm) and grow on short, delicate stalks. However, a single plant may cover a considerable area. Flowers May–September.

329 Are the leaves composite?

(from 323)

Answer 'Yes' if each leaf is composed of several separate leaflets. Answer 'No' if the leaves, though they may be deeply divided, are each single and independent.

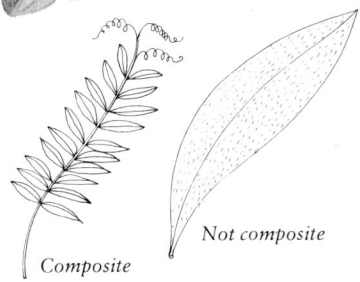

Yes 330 No 331

330 TUFTED VETCH
(Vicia cracca)

(from 329)

This is much the bluest of the common vetches and grows to the greatest size. Using its twisty tendrils, it may climb and clamber for up to 200cm over surrounding vegetation. The flowers are in long clusters of up to 40 blooms, all facing more or less the same way. Each leaf is divided into 8–12 pairs of opposite leaflets, and grows on a short stalk from the weak, twining stem. The whole plant is slightly hairy. Tufted vetch grows in hedgerows, scrubland and open woodland. Flowers June–August.

331 How big are the flowers?

(from 329)
Measure the diameter of an average flower and choose your answer accordingly.

Over 10mm 332
Under 10mm 333

332 VIPER'S-BUGLOSS
(Echium vulgare)

(from 331)

The bright blue flowers (10–20mm) are extremely conspicuous. They grow in a loose spike and have 5 irregular petals, fused together to form a tube. The plant grows erect and is covered in pale bristly hairs. The leaves are narrow and very pointed. Viper's-bugloss always grows on dry ground and prefers grassland; also found on cliffs and sand dunes. Flowers June–September.

333 COMMON MILKWORT
(Polygala vulgaris)

(from 331)

This little plant has very small, bright blue flowers (6–8mm), arranged in long clusters at the ends of its branched stems. The leaves are also very small; they are narrow, pointed and without teeth or stalks. Usually found in grassland. Flowers May–June.

334 Do the flowers have 4 distinct petals?

(from 322)

Answer 'Yes' if each flower has 4 distinct petals, all nearly (but not quite) the same size. Answer 'No' if the flowers are much more irregular, with or without a single upper lip and with a 3-lobed lower lip.

Yes 335 No 336

4 distinct petals

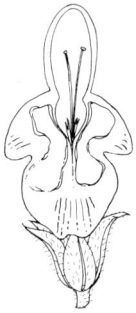

3-lobed lower lip

335

(from 334)

GERMANDER SPEEDWELL
(Veronica chamaedrys)
BROOKLIME
(Veronica beccabunga)

These two related species are quite similar and it is best to take them together. In both cases the upper petal is slightly larger, the lower slightly smaller than the 2 others. Speedwell's flowers (10mm) are somewhat bigger than brooklime's (5–8mm) and a rather paler blue. Moreover the latter is always hairless, while the leaves and stems of the former are noticeably hairy. Brooklime, which flowers May–September, prefers a damp site, usually near water; germander speedwell (March–July) grows in dry grassland, woods and hedgerows.

Germander speedwell

Brooklime

336 Is much of the stem creeping?

(from 334)

Answer 'Yes' if much of the stem is lying prostrate along the ground, rising from it to bear the leaves and flowers. Answer 'No' if the whole plant stands erect.

Yes 337 No 338

337

GROUND-IVY
(Glechoma hederacea)

(from 336)

Ground-ivy is a creeping plant with rooting stems, rising at their extremities to bear leaves and flowers. The whole plant is slightly hairy. The mauve or pink flowers, up to 2cm long, grow in pairs in the leaf axils (the points where the leaf-stalks join the stems). The long-stalked leaves are rounded or kidney-shaped. Ground-ivy usually grows on damp ground in woods and on wasteland. Flowers March–May.

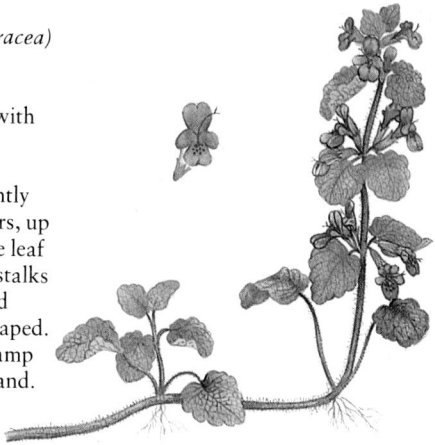

338 Is the flower 2-lipped?

(from 336)

Answer 'Yes' if the flower has a hooded upper lip and a 3-lobed lower lip. Answer 'No' if the upper lip is missing.

Yes 339 No 340

Hooded upper lip

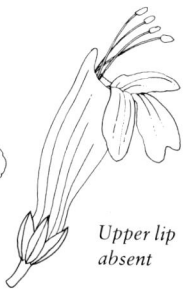

Upper lip absent

339

SELFHEAL
(Prunella vulgaris)

(from 338)

Selfheal bears a superficial resemblance to bugle (see 340); but all or almost all the flowers, which are lighter and more purplish in colour, grow in a single cluster above

Selfheal

Bugle

the top pair of leaves. The leaf-stalks are longest towards the base of the plant; the leaves are oval, pointed and untoothed. Selfheal grows in grassland and woods. Flowers June–September.

340 **BUGLE**
(Ajuga reptans)
(from 338)

Bugle's blue flowers are in diminishing whorls around its erect stem, with a small pair of leaves below each whorl. The number of whorls is very variable, as is the plant's height, which is usually less than 10cm but may reach 30cm or more. Bugle is found in damp meadows, woodland or hedgerows. Flowers April–June.

341 **SWEET VIOLET**
(Viola odorata)
(from 322)

Sweet violet and dog violet (see 325) are the two members of this much-loved family most commonly seen in Britain. They are most easily told apart by the sweet violet's smell, and its heart-shaped leaves which all rise from the base of the plant, not alternately along the stems. Each delicate flower-stalk bears a single flower. Sweet violet grows in woodlands and hedgerows. Flowers March–May.

342 Is the plant growing in water?

(from 1)
Answer 'Yes' if the lower part of the stem, or all the stem, is submerged in water. Answer 'No' if the plant is growing on dry land, or if only the roots are submerged.

Yes 343 No 350

343 Are the leaves very long and narrow?

(from 342)
Answer 'Yes' if all the leaves grow erect and are long and narrow, like those of a reed or iris. Otherwise answer 'No'.

Yes 344 No 347

344 Do the flowers grow in a dense spike?

(from 343)
Answer 'Yes' if the very small flowers grow in a dense, erect spike, which rises vertically above the water. Otherwise answer 'No'.

Yes 345 No 346

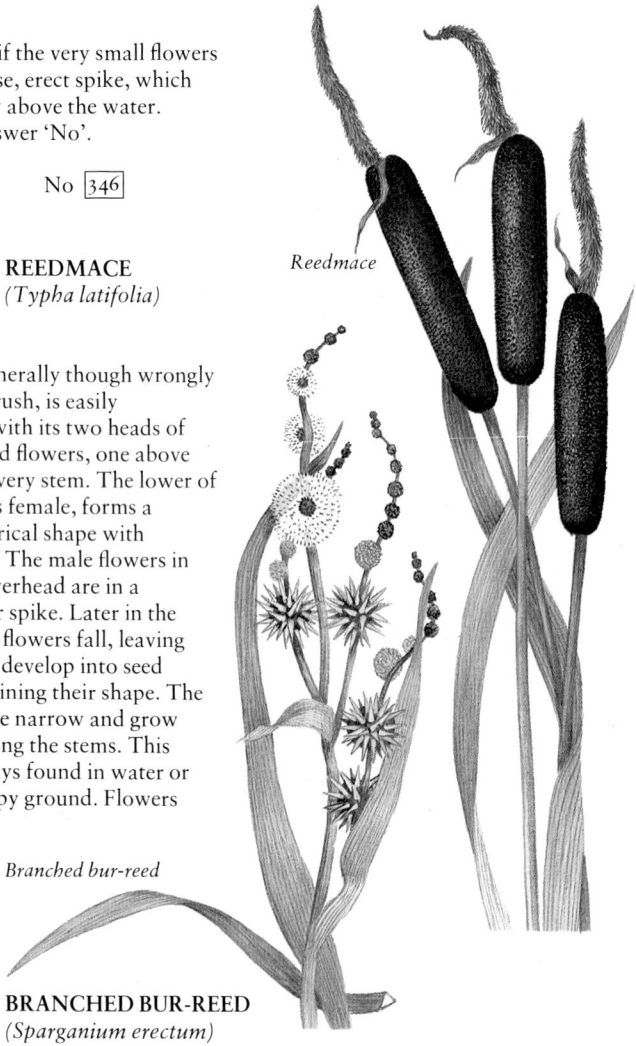

Reedmace

Branched bur-reed

345 REEDMACE
(Typha latifolia)

(from 344)

Reedmace, generally though wrongly known as bulrush, is easily recognizable with its two heads of densely-packed flowers, one above the other on every stem. The lower of these, which is female, forms a regular cylindrical shape with rounded ends. The male flowers in the upper flowerhead are in a smaller, looser spike. Later in the year, the male flowers fall, leaving the females to develop into seed while still retaining their shape. The leaves are quite narrow and grow alternately along the stems. This species is always found in water or on very swampy ground. Flowers June–July.

346 BRANCHED BUR-REED
(Sparganium erectum)

(from 344)

The tiny flowers grow in rounded flowerheads at the ends of the branched stems, which also bear leaves. The smaller flowerheads at the top of the stem are male, the larger ones below them are female. The main leaves grow from the base of the plant, which is normally submerged in water. Flowers June–August.

347 Do the flowers grow in a dense spike?

(from 343)

Answer 'Yes' if the flowers grow in a conspicuous spike. Answer 'No' if they grow singly and are extremely hard to find.

Yes 348 No 349

Flowers in spike

348 BROAD-LEAVED PONDWEED

(Potamogeton natans)

(from 347)

The dense spikes (3–8cm long) of tiny green flowers make this plant quite easy to recognize. It has broad, leathery, pointed leaves floating on the surface of the water, as well as narrow ones below it, which may not be visible. This pondweed grows in still water or slow-moving rivers. Flowers May–September.

349 COMMON WATER-STARWORT

(Callitriche stagnalis)

(from 347)

The flowers are so tiny, without petals or sepals, that you are quite likely not to notice them. They grow in the leaf axils (the points where the leaves join the stem). The shape of the hairless leaves is variable, either strap-shaped or oval. They float on the water or are just below the surface. Mostly they are in opposite pairs but sometimes they grow in whorls. Water-starwort grows in still or slow-moving water, occasionally on wet mud beside it. Flowers May–September.

350 How do the leaves grow?

(from 342)

Leaves are described as being alternate, opposite or basal depending on how they are arranged along their stem or stalk. The drawings will help you to decide.

Alternate leaves grow singly, on alternating sides of the stem. Opposite leaves are in pairs. Choose 'basal only' if all the leaves grow at the very base of the plant.

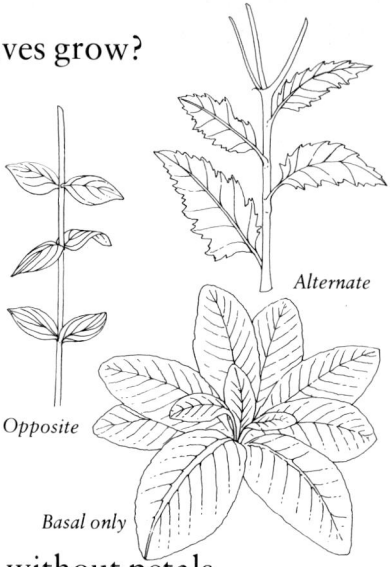

Alternate 351
Opposite 364
Basal only 369

351 Are the flowers without petals or sepals?

(from 350)

Answer 'Yes' if the little green flowers are quite without petals or sepals. They consist only of an ovary and stamens, though beneath these is a circle of leaf-like bracts, which might be mistaken for part of the flower. Answer 'No' if the plant quite clearly has petals or sepals, though they may be very small.

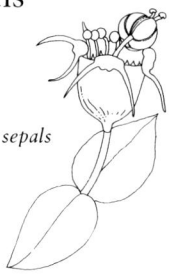

Yes 352 No 353

352

(from 351)

PETTY SPURGE
(Euphorbia peplus)
SUN SPURGE
(Euphorbia helioscopia)

These two spurges are similar and it is best to take them together. They are difficult species because the flowers are so tiny that you might not think they are in bloom. In sun spurge, the bracts (see 351) are yellowish and grow in whorls under the flowers. In the petty spurge they are greener and tend to be opposite.

363

(from 359)

FAT-HEN
(Chenopodium album)
COMMON ORACHE
(Atriplex patula)

These two plants are similar and it is best to take them together. The main distinction is that the orache has different male and female flowers, whilst fat-hen's flowers are all the same. In both cases, the spikes of flowers rise from the leaf axils (where the leaves join the stem). Fat-hen's stem is very often reddish. The leaves are very variable. Both plants are found on cultivated ground or wasteland. Flower July–September, the fat-hen till October.

364

(from 350)

Does the plant grow upright?

Answer 'Yes' if it grows with an upright, self-supporting stem. Answer 'No' if most of the stems are lying along the ground, rising only towards their extremities.

Yes 365 No 368

Stems not upright

Upright stem

365

(from 364)

Are the flowers in hanging spikes?

Answer 'Yes' if the tiny flowers grow in long, hanging spikes. Answer 'No' if the spikes are upright.

Yes 366 No 367

359 Is the plant a climber?

(from 357)

Answer 'Yes' if it grows by twining itself around other vegetation or clinging to it. Answer 'No' if the stem is upright and self-supporting.

Yes 360 No 363

360 Are the flowers extremely small?

(from 359)

Answer 'Yes' if the flowers are tiny – no more than 5mm in diameter

Answer 'No' if they exceed 10mm.

Yes 361 No 362

361 IVY *(Hedera helix)*

(from 360)

Ivy's flowers are often extremely difficult to find because, apart from being so small, they grow only on the uppermost part of the plant, which may climb to a height of over 30m. They are in small rounded clusters, which become more conspicuous when the bright green berries develop, and later turn black. Ivy, with its woody stem and deeply lobed leaves, is well-known on trees almost everywhere. Flowers September–November.

362 WHITE BRYONY *(Bryonia dioica)*

(from 360 and 124)

The male flowers (12–18mm) grow on stalks in small clusters. The female flowers are smaller and very inconspicuous, till they turn to red berries. The leaves are very deeply lobed. Twining tendrils grow directly from the angled stem, enabling the plant to clamber over surrounding vegetation. Usually found in hedgerows and woodland. Flowers May–September.

356 **BROAD-LEAVED DOCK**
(Rumex obtusifolia)

(from 354)

This unbeautiful flower is a common farmland weed and also grows on wasteland. The tiny flowers have 6 sepals and no petals; they grow in whorls. The stem is branched and tends to be tinged with red, as do the seeds when they ripen. The leaves are fairly broad, with pointed or rounded tips, and may grow to a great size – up to 25cm in length. Their undersides may be hairy. Flowers June–October.

357 How many petals has each flower?

(from 353)

Count the number of petals in each flower and choose your answer accordingly.

4 358
5 359
6 139

358 **LADY'S-MANTLE**
(Alchemilla vulgaris)

(from 357)

The tiny green flowers (3–5mm) have no true petals, but 4 petal-like, pointed sepals. They grow in small clusters at the ends of the branched stems. The toothed leaves grow mainly at the base of the plant; they are quite deeply lobed and have long stalks. Others, which are more rounded, grow alternately along the stem and are stalkless. Grows in grassland, usually meadows. Flowers June–September.

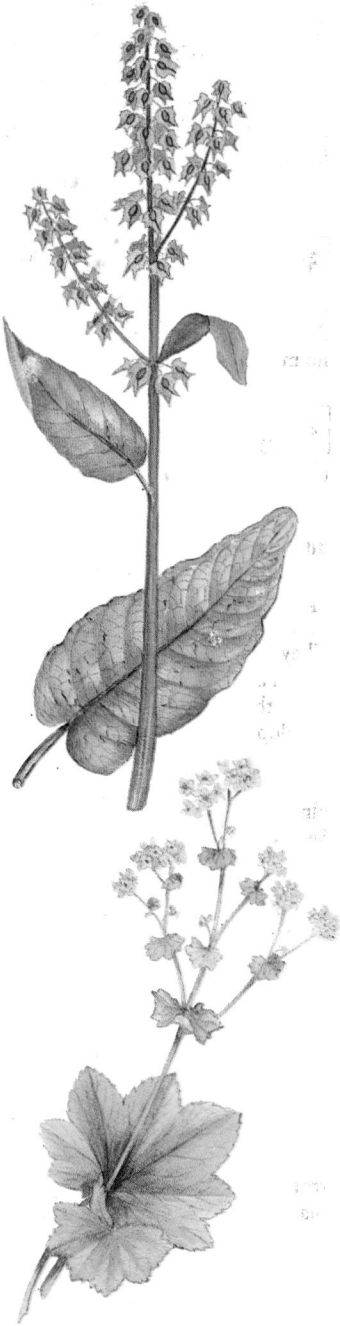

Both species are erect and hairless. Sun spurge reaches a greater height (50cm) and has stalkless leaves; petty spurge's leaves have short stalks and the plant does not exceed 30cm. Both are found on arable ground and wasteland. Petty spurge flowers April–November, sun spurge May–October.

Sun spurge

353

(from 351)

Do the flowers have 6 sepals and no petals?

Examine the flowers very carefully. Those of the dock and sorrel, which are extremely small, have 6 sepals and no petals. Three of these sepals are so tiny that you may not notice them at first. The other three are petal-like, till they fall as the seeds ripen and turn red. Answer 'Yes' if your plant is one of these. Otherwise answer 'No'.

Yes 354 No 357

354

(from 353)

Do the leaves have an acid taste?

Chew one of the leaves. Answer 'Yes' if it tastes distinctly acid or sour. Otherwise answer 'No'.

Yes 355 No 356

355

(from 354)

COMMON SORREL
(Rumex acetosa)

The leaves are long and narrow, with pointed lobes at their bases. Those towards the base have long stalks, but the upper ones are stalkless. The little green flowers, which become tinged with red, are in loose whorls around the branched stems. Common sorrel is hairless and grows upright. As the summer goes by, the whole plant tends to turn red. It grows in grassland, woodland and on waste ground. Flowers May–June.

366 COMMON NETTLE
(Urtica dioica)

(from 365)

Almost everyone knows the rightly unpopular nettle, with its pointed, stinging leaves, which grow in opposite pairs and are noticeably toothed. The tiny flowers are in dangling spikes growing in the leaf axils (the points where the leaves join the stem). Nettles grow mainly on wasteland and in woods. Flowers June–August.

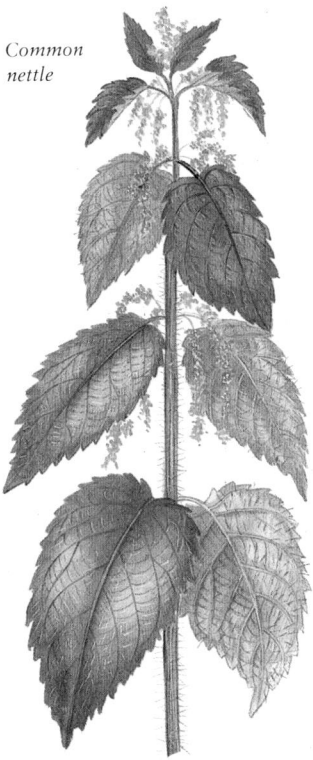

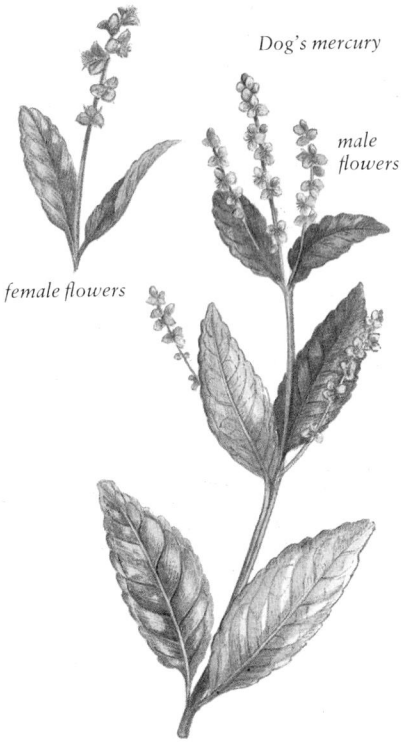

367 DOG'S MERCURY
(Mercurialis perennis)

(from 365)

Plants of this species are either male or female. In both cases, the little green flowers are very inconspicuous. Both sexes have 3 regular, pointed, petal-like sepals. The male flowers have yellow stamens in the centres; they grow in long upright spikes from the leaf-axils (where the leaves join the stems). The females are smaller and even less noticeable, on 3cm stalks in groups of 1–3. The leaves are hairy, oval and pointed. Dog's mercury usually grows in woodland. Flowers February–April.

368 (from 364)

PROCUMBENT PEARLWORT
(Sagina procumbens)

This is such a small plant, with tiny flowers (4mm) and small, very narrow leaves, that it often escapes attention. The flowers normally have no true petals, but 4 pointed petal-like sepals. They grow on stalks rising from procumbent runners, which spread along the ground from a central rosette of leaves. Pearlwort usually grows on lawns, other grassy places or pathways. Flowers June–August.

369 (from 350)

Are the flowers arranged in a loose spike?

Answer 'Yes' if the orchid-like flowers are in a loose spike, all facing much the same way, along the upper half of the stem. Otherwise answer 'No'.

Yes 370

No 371

Flowers in loose spike

370 (from 369)

COMMON TWAYBLADE
(Listera ovata)

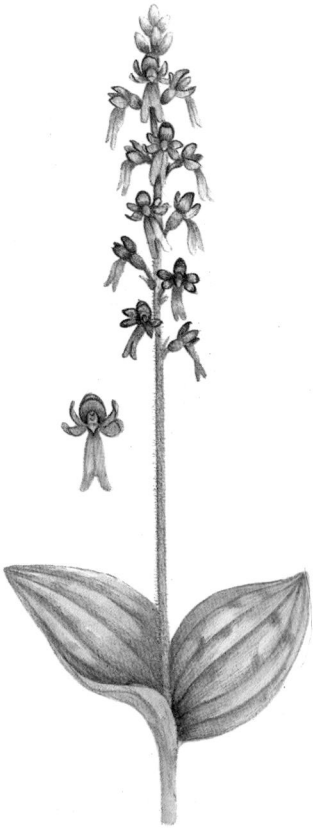

This is a member of the orchid family and has distinctive orchid-like flowers in a loose spike at the top of its single stem. It is also easily recognized by the broad, opposite leaves, which grow in a pair (never more) near the base of the stem. Twayblade is found in damp woods and grassland. It flowers June–July.

371 Are the leaves narrow?

(from 369)
Answer 'Yes' if the leaf is at least 5 times as long as it is wide. Answer 'No' if it is not more than 3 times as long as it is wide.

Yes 372 No 373

372 RIBWORT PLANTAIN
(Plantago lanceolata)

(from 371)

This is the very well-known plantain that grows everywhere in fields, lawns and other grassland. It can be confused only with the greater plantain (see 373), whose spike of tiny flowers is longer and greener. The ribwort plantain also has much narrower leaves. Flowers April–October.

373 GREATER PLANTAIN
(Plantago major)

(from 371)

The flowers are in long green spikes at the ends of stems which rise upright from the rosette of leaves at the base. The spikes are much longer, the leaves less narrow and the stems usually shorter than in the case of the better known ribwort plantain (see 372). Usually grows in fields and other grassy places. Flowers June–October.

1986

Index and Checklist

Use the boxes to mark with an 'x' each new species as you see it. There are spare boxes at the end for you to insert other species that are not included in the book.

ENGLISH NAMES

- ☐ Aaron's-rod 41
- ☐ Agrimony, Common 30
- Agrimony, Hemp *see* Hemp-agrimony
- ☐ Angelica, Wild 100
- ☐ Anemone, Wood 146
- ☐ Arrowhead 285
- ☐ Asphodel, Bog 80
- ☐ Aster, Sea 318
- ☐ Avens, Water 237

- ☐ Bilberry 215
- ☐ Bindweed, Black 125
- ☐ Bindweed, Field 212
- ☐ Bindweed, Hedge 113
- ☐ Bistort, Amphibious 247
- ☐ Bittersweet 313
- ☐ Bladderwort, Greater 5
- ✓ Bluebell 302 6/12
- ☐ Bogbean 288
- ☐ Bramble 229
- ☐ Brooklime 335
- ☐ Bryony, Black 139
- ☐ Bryony, White 362
- ☐ Bugle 340
- ☐ Burdock, Lesser 204
- ☐ Burnet-saxifrage 109
- ☐ Bur-reed, Branched 346
- ☐ Butterbur 290
- ☐ Buttercup, Creeping 37
- ☐ Buttercup, Meadow 37

- ☐ Campion, Bladder 158
- ☐ Campion, Red 273
- ☐ Campion, White 157
- ☐ Carrot, Wild 103
- ☐ Cat's-ear 82
- ☐ Celandine, Greater 21
- ☐ Celandine, Lesser 74
- ☐ Centaury, Common 270
- ☐ Charlock 25
- ☐ Chickweed 155
- ☐ Clover, Red 206
- ☐ Clover, White 185
- ☐ Colt's-foot 86
- ☐ Comfrey, Common 114
- ☐ Cowslip 77
- ☐ Crane's-bill, Meadow 315
- ☐ Cuckoo flower 310

- ☐ Daffodil, Wild 79
- ☐ Daisy 182
- ☐ Daisy, Ox-eye 137
- ☐ Dandelion 84
- ☐ Dead-nettle, Red 279
- ☐ Dead-nettle, White 169
- ☐ Dock, Broad-leaved 356

- ☐ Enchanter's-nightshade 168
- ☐ Eyebright 170

- ☐ Fat-hen 363
- ☐ Figwort, Common 277
- ☐ Flax, Fairy 165
- ☐ Flowering-rush 283
- ✓ Forget-me-not, Field 316 6/12
- ☐ Foxglove 210
- ☐ Fumitory, Common 224

- ☐ Gentian, Field 311
- ☐ Goldenrod 42
- ☐ Goosegrass 145
- ☐ Goutweed 99
- ☐ Grass-of-Parnassus 181
- ☐ Ground-ivy 337
- ☐ Groundsel, Common 11

- ☐ Harebell 304
- ☐ Hawkbit, Autumnal 85
- ☐ Hawk's-beard, Smooth 49
- ☐ Hawkweed 48

- [ ] Heath, Cross-leaved 262
- [ ] Heather 264
- [ ] Heather, Bell 262
- [ ] Helleborine, Broad-leaved 249
- [ ] Hemlock 105
- [ ] Hemp-agrimony 259
- [ ] Hemp-nettle, Common 280
- [ ] Herb bennet 40
- [x] Herb-robert 239 6/12
- [ ] Hogweed 97
- Holly, Sea *see* Sea-holly
- [ ] Honeysuckle 70

- [ ] Iris, Yellow 16
- [ ] Ivy 361
- Ivy, Ground *see* Ground-ivy

- [ ] Jack-go-to-bed-at-noon 44

- [ ] Knapweed, Common 203
- [ ] Knotgrass 131

- [ ] Lady's-bedstraw 61
- [ ] Lady's-mantle 358
- [ ] Lily-of-the-valley 190
- [ ] Loosestrife, Purple 274
- [ ] Lords-and-ladies 183

- [ ] Madder, Field 307
- [ ] Mallow, Common 241
- [ ] Marsh-marigold 33
- [ ] Mayweed, Scentless 136
- [ ] Meadowsweet 128
- [ ] Medick, Black 56
- [ ] Mercury, Dog's 367
- [ ] Milkwort, Common 333
- [ ] Mint, Corn 321
- [ ] Mint, Water 320
- [ ] Mouse-ear, Common 154
- [ ] Mugwort 10
- [ ] Mustard, Garlic 118
- [ ] Mustard, Hedge 26

- [ ] Nettle, Common 366
- [ ] Nipplewort 49

- [ ] Orache, Common 363
- [ ] Orchid, Common spotted 253
- [ ] Orchid, Early purple 254
- [ ] Orchid, Fragrant 251
- [ ] Orchid, Greater Butterfly 140
- [ ] Orpine 243

- [ ] Pansy, Wild 327
- [ ] Parsley, Cow 108
- [ ] Parsley, Upright hedge 106
- [ ] Pearlwort, Procumbent 368
- [ ] Pimpernel, Scarlet 269
- [ ] Pimpernel, Yellow 63
- [ ] Pineappleweed 14
- [ ] Plantain, Greater 373
- [ ] Plantain, Ribwort 372
- Plantain, Water *see* Water-plantain
- [ ] Pondweed, Broad-leaved 348
- [ ] Poppy, Common 219
- [ ] Poppy, Yellow horned 24
- [ ] Poppy, Long-headed 220
- [ ] Primrose 76

- [ ] Radish, Wild 117
- [ ] Ragged-robin 272
- [ ] Ragwort, Common 50
- [ ] Ramsons 191
- [ ] Rattle, Red 214
- [ ] Rattle, Yellow 72
- [ ] Redshank 245
- [ ] Reedmace 345
- [ ] Restharrow 234
- [ ] Rocket, Sea 222
- [ ] Rose, Burnet 122
- [ ] Rose, Dog 230
- Rush, Flowering *see* Flowering-rush

- [ ] St John's-wort, Perforate 66
- [ ] St John's-wort, Square-stemmed 65
- [ ] Sandwort, Sea 164
- [ ] Sandwort, Thyme-leaved 162
- Saxifrage, Burnet *see* Burnet-saxifrage
- [ ] Saxifrage, Rue-leaved 133
- [ ] Scabious, Devil's-bit 296
- [ ] Scabious, Field 297
- [ ] Sea-holly 294

- [ ] Selfheal 339
- [ ] Shepherd's-purse 119
- [ ] Silverweed 29
- [ ] Snowdrop 174
- [ ] Sorrel, Common 355
- [ ] Sow-thistle, Smooth 46
- [ ] Spearwort, Lesser 34
- [ ] Speedwell, Germander 335
- [ ] Spurge, Petty 352
- [ ] Spurge, Sun 352
- [ ] Spurrey, Corn 160
- [ ] Spurrey, Sand 267
- [ ] Starwort, Common water 349
- [ ] Stitchwort, Lesser 150
- [ ] Stitchwort, Greater 151
- [ ] Stonecrop, Biting 39
- [ ] Stork's-bill, Common 238
- [ ] Strawberry, Barren 179
- [x] Strawberry, Wild 178 6/12
- [ ] Sundew, Round-leaved 187

- [ ] Tansy 13
- [ ] Thistle, Creeping 201
- [ ] Thistle, Marsh 199
- [ ] Thistle, Spear 197
- [ ] Thistle, Welted 200
- [ ] Thrift 291
- [ ] Toadflax, Common 58
- [ ] Toadflax, Ivy-leaved 328
- [ ] Tormentil 22
- [ ] Traveller's-joy 144
- [ ] Trefoil, Bird's-foot 55
- [ ] Twayblade, Common 370

- [ ] Valerian, Common 258
- [ ] Vetch, Bush 232
- [ ] Vetch, Common 232
- [ ] Vetch, Kidney 53
- [ ] Vetch, Tufted 330
- [ ] Vetchling, Meadow 68
- [ ] Violet, Common dog 325
- [ ] Violet, Sweet 341
- [ ] Viper's-bugloss 332

- [ ] Water-crowfoot, Thread-leaved 91
- [ ] Water-lily, White 92
- [ ] Water-lily, Yellow 4
- [ ] Water-plantain 286
- [ ] Waterweed, Canadian 90
- [ ] Willowherb, Broad-leaved 265
- [ ] Willowherb, Great 265
- [ ] Willowherb, Rosebay 225
- [ ] Wood-sorrel 180
- [ ] Woundwort, Hedge 280

- [ ] Yarrow 129

- [ ] .....
- [ ] .....
- [ ] .....
- [ ] .....
- [ ] .....
- [ ] .....
- [ ] .....
- [ ] .....
- [ ] .....
- [ ] .....

SCIENTIFIC NAMES

Achillea millefolium 129
Aegopodium podagraria 99
Agrimonia eupatoria 30
Ajuga reptans 340
Alchemilla vulgaris 358
Alisma plantago-aquatica 286
Alliaria petiolata 118
Allium ursinum 191
Anagallis arvensis 269
Anemone nemorosa 146
Angelica sylvestris 100
Anthriscus sylvestris 108
Anthyllis vulneraria 53
Arctium minus 204
Arenaria serpyllifolia 162
Armeria maritima 291
Artemisia vulgaris 10
Arum maculatum 183
Aster tripolium 318
Atriplex patula 363

Bellis perennis 182
Bryonia dioica 362
Butomus umbellatus 283

Cakile maritima 222
Callitriche stagnalis 349
Calluna vulgaris 264
Caltha palustris 33
Calystegia sepium 113
Campanula rotundifolia 304
Capsella bursa-pastoris 119
Cardamine pratensis 310
Carduus acanthoides 200
Centaurea nigra 203
Centaurium erythraea 270
Cerastium fontanum 154
Chelidonium majus 21
Chenopodium album 363
Circaea lutetiana 168
Cirsium arvense 201
  palustre 199
  vulgare 197
Clematis vitalba 144
Conium maculatum 105
Convallaria majalis 190
Convolvulus arvensis 212
Crepis capillaris 49
Cymbalaria muralis 328

Dactylorhiza fuchsii 253
Daucus carota 103
Digitalis purpurea 210
Drosera rotundifolia 187

Echium vulgare 332
Elodea canadensis 90
Epilobium angustifolium 225
  hirsutum 265
  montanum 265
Epipactis helleborine 249
Erica cinerea 262
  tetralix 262
Erodium cicutarium 238
Eryngium maritimum 294
Eupatorium cannabinum 259
Euphorbia helioscopia 352
  peplus 352
Euphrasia nemorosa 170

Fallopia convolvulus 125
Filipendula ulmaria 128
Fragaria vesca 178
Fumaria officinalis 224

Galanthus nivalis 174
Galeopsis tetrahit 280
Galium aparine 145
  verum 61
Gentianella campestris 311
Geranium pratense 315
  robertianum 239
Geum rivale 237
  urbanum 40
Glaucium flavum 24
Glechoma hederacea 337
Gymnadenia conopsea 251

Hedera helix 361
Heracleum sphondylium 97
Hieracium 48
Honkenya peploides 164
Hyacinthoides non-scripta 302
Hypericum perforatum 66
  tetrapterum 65
Hypochoeris radicata 82

Iris pseudacorus 16

Knautia arvensis 297

Lamium album 169
  purpureum 279
Lapsana communis 49
Lathyrus pratensis 68
Leontodon autumnalis 85
Leucanthemum vulgare 137
Linaria vulgaris 58
Linum catharticum 165
Listera ovata 370
Lonicera periclymenum 70
Lotus corniculatus 55
Lychnis flos-cuculi 272
Lysimachia nemorum 63
Lythrum salicaria 274

Malva sylvestris 241
Matricaria matricarioides 14
Medicago lupulina 56
Mentha aquatica 320
  arvensis 321
Menyanthes trifoliata 288
Mercurialis perennis 367
Myosotis arvensis 316

Narcissus pseudonarcissus 79
Narthecium ossifragum 80
Nuphar lutea 4
Nymphaea alba 92

Ononis repens 234
Orchis mascula 254
Oxalis acetosella 180

Papaver dubium 220
rhoeas 219
Parnassia palustris 181
Pedicularis palustris 214
Petasites hybridus 290
Pimpinella saxifraga 109
Plantago lanceolata 372
major 373
Platanthera chlorantha 140
Polygala vulgaris 333
Polygonum amphibium 247
aviculare 131
persicaria 245
Potamogeton natans 348
Potentilla anserina 29
erecta 22
sterilis 179
Primula veris 77
vulgaris 76
Prunella vulgaris 339

Ranunculus acris 37
ficaria 74
flammula 34
repens 37
trichophyllus 91
Raphanus raphanistrum 117
Rhinanthus minor 72
Rosa canina 230
pimpinellifolia 122
Rubus fruticosus 229
Rumex acetosa 355
obtusifolia 356

Sagina procumbens 368
Sagittaria sagittifolia 285
Saxifraga tridactylites 133
Scrophularia nodosa 277
Sedum acre 39
telephium 243
Senecio jacobaea 50
vulgaris 11
Sherardia arvensis 307
Silene alba 157
dioica 273
vulgaris 158
Sinapis arvensis 25
Sisymbrium officinale 26
Solanum dulcamara 313
Solidago virgaurea 42
Sonchus oleraceus 46
Sparganium erectum 346
Spergula arvensis 160
Spergularia rubra 267
Stachys sylvatica 280
Stellaria graminea 150
holostea 151
media 155
Succisa pratensis 296
Symphytum officinale 114

Tamus communis 139
Tanacetum vulgare 13
Taraxacum officinale 84
Torilis japonica 106
Tragopogon pratensis 44
Trifolium pratense 206
repens 185
Tripleurospermum inodorum 136
Tussilago farfara 86
Typha latifolia 345

Urtica dioica 366
Utricularia vulgaris 5

Vaccinium myrtillus 215
Valeriana officinalis 258
Verbascum thapsus 41
Veronica beccabunga 335
chamaedrys 335
Vicia cracca 330
sativa 232
sepium 232
Viola odorata 341
riviniana 325
tricolor 327